Secrets Of The Hunting Pros

Secrets Of The Hunting Pros

Hunter's Information Series™
North American Hunting Club
Minneapolis, Minnesota

Secrets Of The Hunting Pros

Copyright © 1993, North American Hunting Club

All rights reserved.

Library of Congress Catalog Card Number 92-83733
ISBN 0-914697-54-4

Printed in U.S.A.
   2   3   4   5   6   7   8   9

The North American Hunting Club
offers a line of hats for hunters.
For information, write:
    North American Hunting Club
    P.O. Box 3401
    Minneapolis, MN 55343

Contents

Acknowledgments

The North American Hunting Club would like to thank everyone who helped create this book.

Artist David Rottinghaus provided all illustrations. Aside from the authors' contributions for their own chapters, the following supplied photos or materials: Mike Biggs, Glenn Chambers, Len Clifford, Judd Cooney, Pat Costello, Paul DeMarchi, *North American Hunter* Senior Editor Dan Dietrich, The Farrell Group, Federal Cartridge Company, Larry Frisoli, *North American Hunter* Publisher Mark LaBarbera, Hunter's Information Series Managing Editor Ron Larsen, Pat Meitin, *North American Hunter* Editor Bill Miller, Neal and Mary Jane Mishler, Operation Orphans, Remington Arms Company, Inc., Len Rue Jr., Leonard Lee Rue III, Leonard Lee Rue IV, Dwight Schuh, Hal Swiggett and Bill Vaznis.

A special thanks to the North American Hunting Club's publications staff for all their efforts: Publisher Mark LaBarbera, Editor Bill Miller, Managing Editor of Books Ron Larsen, Senior Editor Dan Dietrich, Associate Editor of Books Colleen Ferguson and Editorial Assistant Victoria Brouillette. Thanks also to Vice President of Product Marketing Mike Vail, Assistant Vice President/Marketing Manager Cal Franklin and Marketing Project Coordinator Laura Resnik.

Foreword

Becoming "the best" at something requires experience and effort. Reading the NAHC Hunter's Information Series, viewing in-depth videos on the finer points of the sport and following in the footsteps of fathers and grandfathers, no doubt, will launch you far into a memorable hunting career. But until you've actually "been there," everything you've learned is usually nothing more than theory. Hands-on, in-the-field, dirt-under-your-fingernails experience is the ingredient that makes great hunters.

You'll find there is no "theory" between the covers of this Hunter's Information Series title, *Secrets Of The Hunting Pros*. This book contains rock-solid advice and documented discoveries from some of the world's most knowledgeable and experienced hunters, shooters and outdoor writers. Their combined experiences on every conceivable aspect of hunting equals many lifetimes. NAHC handgunning expert Hal Swiggett alone accounts for more than 65 years of actual shooting and hunting experience! NAHC Shooting Advisory Council member Larry L. Weishuhn has been referred to as "Mr. Whitetail" and "the most knowledgeable deer hunter in North America."

As you read this compilation of incredible shared knowledge and experiences, there will be some authors' names you recognize and others you won't. For example, Hal Swiggett, Larry L. Weishuhn, Don Zutz and Chuck Adams are names that carry a lot of weight in hunting and shooting circles. You've seen their work for many years in *North*

American Hunter magazine and other publications. Other hunters like Bill Hanus, Ron Doss and Tony Caligiuri aren't as well-known, but were sought out especially for this project because of their extensive backgrounds and field research in the areas about which they've written. We've also included chapters from NAHC staff members Mark LaBarbera and Bill Miller who have gained special insights on hunting from their travels for *North American Hunter* magazine and for the "North American Outdoors" television series.

It seems fitting for the North American Hunting Club to publish a book like *Secrets Of The Hunting Pros*. With more than 500,000 Members generously sharing the exciting news of their hunting successes, we have the resources to ferret out the latest and most effective techniques to improve your hunting skills and success. As we outlined the topics for the chapters in the book, we asked ourselves, "Of all the hunting writers we know, who knows the most about ... ?" Then it was simply contacting the right people and putting their secrets down on paper.

That kind of access to the best information has produced a book that will be of immeasurable value to hunters of all skill levels. For example, Bill Miller's advice to ask questions first and shoot later when hunting waterfowl can be equally applied by the grizzled veteran duck hunter or the beginner who is just "getting his feet wet" in the hunting tradition. Weishuhn's thoughts and tips on using hunting optics will be beneficial, whether you're buying gear for the first time or upgrading an existing setup. Caligiuri's sage advice on scouting for game may lead you to a trophy that you might otherwise have overlooked.

These are just a few examples of the information you'll find in *Secrets Of The Hunting Pros*. Gathering so much "brass tacks" hunting information from so many sung and unsung hunting heroes was exciting and educational. We're proud to present it to you, our Members, in this book.

Steven F. Burke
President
North American Hunting Club

1

Choosing Rifle Ammunition
by John J. Woods

After choosing the most appropriate cartridge-and-rifle combination for a hunting situation, selecting the correct ammunition is the most important task. Bullet placement remains a paramount consideration. Accurate bullet delivery is crucial.

Even with a perfect rifle, scope, caliber and ammunition setup, you still need to put the bullet in the killing zone. Sufficient shooting practice and confidence in the equipment and component choices you have made should help deliver a bullet on target in the most efficient and humane way possible.

Several years ago, I had to choose rifle, ammo and gear for a Nevada mule-deer hunt. I thought I was planning well in advance, but I learned one, well, maybe two, critical lessons before it was all over.

A few months before the hunt I had purchased a new Ruger Model 77RLS rifle in .270 Winchester—the lightweight carbine version with open sights. This rifle sports an 18½-inch-barrel—perfect for the mission at hand, I thought. Because I would be climbing mountains for the first time, I wanted a light rifle; however, I also needed ballistic potential to cleanly harvest a mulie at reasonable ranges. I thought the .270 with 130-grain bullets would be nearly ideal.

Aside from choosing ammunition, I ordered a new riflescope for this adventure. Because I continued searching for a few factory-ammunition samples to test in my new rifle, I was not too concerned about learning that the scope I wanted was back-ordered.

A week before my hunting departure date, however, without a scope for my Ruger, and six boxes of different brands of untested factory ammo on the shelf, I began to panic.

It was time to pull an old standby rifle-and-ammo combination out of the gun cabinet. After two short sessions on the range, I felt equipped to take on Nevada's mule deer. Then, the day before I was to leave, my scope arrived. I mounted the scope on the Ruger that afternoon and spent the remaining daylight hours running ammo through the new setup. As luck would have it, the Ruger was a superb shooter; it liked one factory load in particular. In Nevada, only days later, I took my first mule deer.

This, however, is not the way to put together rifle-and-ammo combinations for any hunt, especially a once-in-a-lifetime, out-of-state hunt. I learned two important lessons from this experience: You should never trust mail order for crucial hunting equipment needs unless you order at least six months in advance of your trip, and factory ammo is hard to beat.

The Selection Process

Choosing rifle ammunition can be as simple or complex as you want to make it. Factory ammunition is hard to beat, but handloading allows you to tailor ammo to your own specifications. So, where should the rifle ammunition selection process begin?

According to NAHC Members Keith LaPorte of Hattiesburg, Mississippi, and Mike Cupp of Reno, Nevada, the place to begin is with available literature. You should study the various cartridges under consideration for the hunt, specific information about the animal to be hunted, such as its terrain and behaviors, and recommended hunting strategies.

"First, I read everything possible about the game that I will be hunting," says La Porte. "I learn all I can about its size, strengths and weaknesses. I then select a caliber that will adequately match the game. I take into consideration terrain, distance of shots and habitat. Once I have selected a caliber, I select the proper bullet weight. Ballistics charts will help tremendously with the selection of calibers and bullet weights."

Cupp relayed his strategy: "I read various outdoor magazine articles first, gathering information from expert gun writers and hunters. Then I apply their suggestions and experiences to the game I want to hunt. I factor in the terrain, the longest or most difficult shot I expect to take (or encounter) and the method I will be using to hunt

Cartridge Match: Bullet Weights To Game Size

Cartridge Choice	Big Game (Deer-Sized)	Big Game (Elk, Moose)	Dangerous Game
.240 Wthby Mag.	100+	—	—
.243 Win.	100	—	—
6mm Rem.	100	—	—
.257 Roberts	117+	—	—
.25-06 Rem.	120	—	—
.270 Win.	130-150	130-150	—
.280 Rem.	100-150	150-175	—
7mm-08 Rem.	140	—	—
7mm Mauser	139-150	—	—
7mm Wthby Mag.	140-150	160-175	—
7mm Rem. Mag.	150-175	150-175	—
.30-30 Win.	150-170	—	—
.308 Win.	150-180	150-180	—
.30-06	130-150	150-180	—
.300 Win. Mag.	165-180	180-220	200-225
.300 Wthby Mag.	165-180	180-225	210-225
.338 Win. Mag.	200-210	210-250	250-300
.340 Wthby Mag.	200-210	210-250	250-300

This chart shows various cartridge choices, bullet weights and game sizes. Although not an all-inclusive list, it does give you an idea of what combinations to use, depending upon the game animal you're hunting.

a particular animal. I select specific bullets for their ballistic characteristics. I look for the best combination of potential speed, down-range energy retention and bullet performance after hitting the animal, with the latter being the most important," he continues. "Why reinvent the wheel? If there is information already out there suggesting or recommending caliber choices, bullets and loads for a given game animal, use it."

Bob Redman of Afton, Michigan, selects his ammo easily because of years of practical hunting experience. He has hunted all over the world, including Russia, Spain and New Zealand, and has successfully hunted most major North American animals.

Bob uses his 7mm Rem. Mag. almost exclusively. After years of hunting, he has settled on one combination that has proven itself successful on all his hunts. He uses 160-grain Nosler Partition bullets and Federal Premium factory ammo exclusively.

"I use the Nosler bullet and Federal Premium ammo for any and

Suggested Bullet Energy Requirements for Game Animals*

Game Type	Minimum	Acceptable	Desired
Deer, antelope, sheep, goats	900 ft. lb.	1200 ft. lb.	1500 ft. lb.
Elk, bear to 600 lbs. live weight	1500 ft. lb.	2000 ft. lb	2500 ft. lb.
Large bear, moose	2100 ft. lb.	2800 ft. lb.	3500 ft. lb.

* Bullet energy at range of target impact.

This chart reveals bullet energy for different-sized game animals. It shows minimum, acceptable and desired bullet-energy levels.

all game,'' he says. ''That way I know what my gun will do at various ranges. I have been using this combination for over five years and it works well for me.''

In the final analysis, it's what works in the field, not at the bench, that makes your selection for you.

After a fair amount of research, it should become apparent what calibers work well for particular game animals. In some cases, such as selecting a .30-06 for big bears, you'll want to examine your choices closely. Selecting bullets can be difficult because there are so many choices in the reloading marketplace today. What sits atop a loaded cartridge case is the one ammo component where little error is acceptable. A bullet must hold together well enough for penetration, yet be flexible enough to expand to maximize tissue disruption for a clean kill.

Four factors should be considered in bullet selection: shooting distance, hunting terrain, the animal's physical makeup and the desired bullet performance.

Predicting a potential range of shooting distances (knowing that anything can happen in hunting) is a starting point for building a load that satisfies energy requirements with a bullet that performs adequately at those ranges.

The Premium brand line from Federal ammunition offers a 7mm Rem. Mag. load with long-range, 140-grain Nosler Partition bullets. Four factors should be considered when selecting a bullet: shooting distance, hunting terrain, the animal's physical makeup and desired bullet performance.

Understanding physical characteristics of the game animal you're hunting is also important. Are you hunting a thin-skinned antelope or deer or a heavy-boned and tissue-laden moose? Generally, the bigger and tougher the animal, the heavier and stronger the bullet will need to be.

Practical Ammunition Testing

After selecting several candidates for that just-right rifle ammo, either factory or handloaded, you need to test them in a field setting. That means lots of shooting at the bench!

Once Cupp chooses a particular load, he's off to the range for one of his usual marathon shooting sessions. "I spend many hours at the range zeroing in at 100- and 200-yard targets," he says. "Then I test the trajectory by shooting at 300, 400 and 500 yards until I'm confident knowing the correct holdover for each of those distances.

"My tests for penetration and performance have been under actual hunting conditions. I try to compare real results with results I've read from laboratory testing. I check bullet path and tissue damage. I also attempt to recover the bullet for examination and evaluation," he concludes.

Redman range-tests his ammunition at 200 and 300 yards. He de-

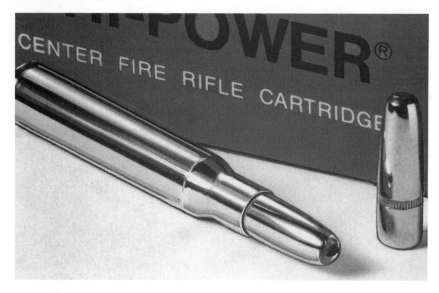

Available in the Federal Cartridge "Hi-Power" line is a .30-06 Springfield cartridge with a 180-grain round-nose, soft-point bullet. This cartridge is good for hunting big game, such as elk or moose.

fers to field experience in making judgments about the success or failure of his ammo selection on game animals. He has not been disappointed yet.

LaPorte says, "I use standard bench-testing methods. I shoot groups of three to five shots, pausing between groups to let the barrel cool down. For penetration and performance I get my test results from the field. I retrieve the bullet, if possible, and retrace the bullet's path to get a better understanding of its route through the animal.

"I also try to take note of the animal's reaction when it's hit to make sure that solid contact was made and to know if a follow-up shot might be needed to dispatch the animal cleanly," he explains.

I follow the same approach as these experienced hunters, but with a high-tech twist. After making my ammo selection, I run the load specs through a ballistics computer program. This program factors in all the essential elements of a load and generates a data screen characterizing the load for me.

The computer program can be set up to provide a complete ballistics profile and the projected trajectory information for various ranges and conditions. It explains the procedure for sighting in a rifle and loading at 25 yards. And, finally, it shows how a particular load will perform at ranges of up to 500 yards.

There has been some controversy about using a 25-yard, sight-in method, but it works for me. Don't get me wrong, I bench-test all my loads extensively at 100 yards, and would use a longer range if available. I can only recall one instance where a load failed to perform as the computer program had predicted at the 100-yard range.

When the rifle and ammunition are fine-tuned, I receive a final computer printout of the load data. Then, I cut out the block of trajectory data and tape it to my riflestock for quick reference in the field. It works great!

Factory Vs. Reloads

With today's advances in the manufacturing technology of factory-based ammunition, it is difficult to argue against its most proven benefits. That being consistency, reliability, accuracy, performance and overall quality.

The flipside to that is cost and, in some cases, less flexibility in bullet choices, or availability of a particular bullet type, design or brand. However, if you consider all the factory offerings on the market today, most hunting situations are covered by one factory ammo or another.

I seldom reload rifle ammo; however, I recognize and respect the advantages of reloading. If you shoot a lot of ammunition, you can save quite a bit of money by investing in reloading equipment and components.

More importantly, the avid handloader benefits from building the exact bullet, powder, primer and brass configuration to use at the range and in the hunting fields. Also, there is no doubt that great personal pleasure can be derived from assembling and testing your own ammunition.

Because of consistent accuracy in his hunting rifles, Bob Redman seldom handloads rifle ammunition. ''I prefer Federal Premium ammo because it offers the bullet I want and a load consistency that has always proven successful in every hunting situation where I have used it,'' he says.

LaPorte chooses factory fodder most of the time, too; however, he still occasionally handloads and uses handloaded ammo on actual hunts. ''I do not reload on a consistent basis,'' he says, ''but I have used handloads on my hunts. Ammunition manufacturers recently began improving their loads, making them more consistent and uniform. Manufacturers are becoming more aware of the demands of hunters for better loads and improved performances.''

Cupp has a different viewpoint: ''Factory loads have come a long

It doesn't take much to start handloading your own accurate ammunition. A reloading press with appropriate dies, a scale, a powder measurer and several reloading manuals should be sufficient.

way in accuracy and reliability, especially the new premium-type loads; however, I still have more options in bullet type and weight, powders and primers when I reload. Therefore, by reloading, I have the ability to fine-tune a particular load to a particular rifle.

"Reloads compare favorably to factory premium loads at a fraction of their price," he continues. "I use reloads exclusively for reasons I've already mentioned, plus I get the satisfaction from knowing I put all the components together myself to achieve my hunting successes. I think it is similar to the satisfaction a fly fisherman gets from tying his own flies and catching fish."

What does John Woods use? I use factory ammunition 99 percent of the time. I can argue all the expected merits of factory ammo with ease, but the main reason I use it is the time factor. Time is a precious commodity, and, unfortunately, I can't justify spending hours at the reloading bench trying to concoct the perfect ammo brew.

I research various factory brands and decide which brands and loads I want to try at the shooting bench. Then, I buy the loads I've selected and shoot a lot to find the one that performs best in my rifle. (When I buy factory ammunition, I usually buy at least two boxes of the same load and brand name. I double-check the inside box flaps to make sure that I'm buying ammunition that comes from identical factory production runs).

Factory Ammo Production Process

John Falk, a respected factory representative from Olin Corporation (Winchester), sent me some excellent information on the production process of fine ammo.

Before any load is mass-produced, it undergoes a series of ballistic tests for velocity, chamber pressure and functioning. Established specifications for the ammo must be met during these tests or adjustments are made and tests are done over.

Once these tests are passed, in-process tests are conducted for bullet extraction, powder weights, dimensional and chamber gaging, visual inspections, incorrect headstamp, component checks, velocity and pressure checks, function tests, accuracy and upset (bullet expansion).

Also, an entire series of lesser-known tests are done such as bullet jump, bullet push, temperature storage tests, water resistance tests and action time (ignition barrel time). Equal testing is also conducted on the individual components.

In the case of most loaded ammunition, over 100 quality checks have been done on the loaded round and the components before any ammunition is packed for distribution. ''Material at any stage of the manufacturing process which does not conform to specification is held and not used in production until corrected,'' Falk says. ''Quality is the most important thing built into our ammunition.''

Choosing rifle ammo is a task easier said than done. There are just too many variables involved to nail down perfection. Therefore, hunters keep going to the reloading table or the shooting bench, searching for yet another ideal load for that upcoming big-game hunt this fall. Isn't that half the fun anyway?

2

Getting The Most From Your Hunting Optics
by Larry L. Weishuhn

Paraphernalia is the passion of many hunters. Collectors of gear and gadgets just aren't content unless they hit the woods loaded down like pack mules. They believe that if one is good, two is better. This chapter is not for gadgeteers. Instead, it examines how to get the most from three basic pieces of modern hunting gear—binoculars, rifle scopes and spotting scopes.

Of all modern hunting equipment available to NAHC Members— other than a bow or firearm—none is more important or basic than good optics!

Binoculars

In relatively open country, binoculars enable the hunter to spot game at long distances, identify the sex and determine its size. Also, the terrain can be scanned to determine how to best stalk or intercept the selected quarry.

For many years, binoculars were the optics of choice only when hunting wide-open country, but now deep-woods hunters are discovering their value. At close ranges, even within 100 yards, binoculars can help determine the source of movement or pick out a set of antlers against a background of branches. Even turkey hunters realize the importance of using binoculars to locate and identify the source of movement seen in the brush.

Quite frankly, as a professional wildlife biologist and fanatical deer hunter, I cannot imagine setting one foot in the field without a good pair of binoculars around my neck!

Binoculars are classified by price, size (pocket, compact, standard or large), magnification, objective lens size, focusing mechanism, and—most importantly—internal design (Poro prism and roof prism).

Poro-prism binoculars are more traditional in design, while roof-prism binoculars are easily identified by their straight tubes. Most optics companies now produce both types. The advantage of roof-prism binoculars is that they are typically smaller and lighter than Poro-prism binoculars of the same magnification.

Following the introduction of Leitz Trinvoid binoculars in 19XX, which greatly improved the roof-prism system, a number of optics companies unveiled similar roof-prism designs. I use Simmons' Gold Medal Series 10X42 binoculars. Like many of the more expensive roof-prism binoculars, they are relatively lightweight and have multi-coated lenses which provide a high-resolution image. I can glass for hours without undue eye strain.

As with the Simmons 10X42, the first number (10) represents the magnification. Thus an object viewed at 1,000 yards would appear 10 times closer. The second number (42) designates the unobstructed diameter of the front or objective lens in millimeters. Generally, the larger the objective lens the more light it will transmit to the eye. Under poor light conditions, a 10X50 will transmit more light to the eye than a 7X35; however, the difference is difficult to detect, except during twilight.

The pupil of the human eye varies in diameter according to light conditions from approximately 2.5mm in size during bright light to around 7mm in total darkness. This relates to the binocular's exit pupil. The larger the exit pupil, the less critical eye alignment becomes. To calculate the figure, divide the objective lens diameter by the magnification. Thus, a 10X42 will have an exit pupil figure of 4.2; a 7X35 an exit pupil of 5.

To illustrate this for yourself, hold your binoculars at arm's length. The little circle you see in each ocular lens is the exit pupil. To be most effective, this number should be between three and five; five or more is even better. If a binocular's exit pupil is approaching five, it will transmit quite a bit of light. However, a 10X binocular will appear brighter than a 7X or 8X binocular because the 10X's higher magnification increases image definition.

This is one of the reasons why the higher magnification and heavier weight binoculars, such as Swarovski's 10X50, and those

Out of all hunting optics available, binoculars are considered the most essential. They are used for glassing terrain to spot and identify game at long distances and to plan your strategy. Binoculars are beneficial in both wide open country and in deep woods.

Binoculars come in two basic internal designs: Poro prism and roof prism. Roof prisms (left) can be identified by their straight tubes, smaller size and lighter weight (at same magnification). Poro prisms (right) are more traditional in design.

produced by Leupold, Bausch & Lomb, Nikon and others of similar size, seem to work well.

Even though many manufacturers stress field of view, serious hunters will probably find this of minor importance when selecting binoculars.

In choosing binoculars, consider how you intend to use them. Will you spend hours glassing from a particular hillside or tree stand? Or will you spend your time still-hunting and crawling in the hills where weight can be a detriment?

For the most part, I use standard-sized binoculars, and have used Poro-prism models, such as 7X35 Bausch & Lomb (made in the early 1950s), 10X42 Simmons and 9X35 Leupold, and the newer roof-prism binoculars. I have found all these to be relatively lightweight, high in quality and versatile—whether hunting in the mountains, on the plains, through the mesquite thickets of south Texas or in the pine forests of the Southeast.

Heavy models, such as the 10X50 Bausch & Lomb and the 10X50 Swarovski SL, are great if you're hunting from a permanent position; however, at 41 and 44 ounces, respectively, I find them a bit heavy to carry all day. There is an advantage to their weight: Heavier binoculars are easier to hold steady when glassing. A hunting companion refers to the latter models as "pickup glasses," because he uses them primarily when scouting from his vehicle.

Personally, I have never found too much use for pocket binoculars. Even their light weight can be more of a detriment than a positive factor. With their small exit-pupil diameter and light weight they are extremely difficult to hold steady. However, they can be advantageous when bowhunting, because they slip easily into a pocket—out of a bowstring's path.

Many of the optics companies produce pocket binoculars, including Simmons, Leupold, Redfield, Bushnell, Tasco and others. The smallest of these is the 7X21 Nichols Poro prism which is 1⅞ inches tall by 4 inches wide and weighs 5½ ounces.

I wear eye glasses so the exit-pupil diameter is very important to me. In selecting a pair of binoculars, I test them to see if a lot of adjustment is needed in order to use them with and without my glasses. When glassing a hillside for a long time, I do not suffer from as much eye strain if I look through binocs without my glasses. However, I normally have them adjusted so I can quickly view what I want to see while wearing my prescription spectacles.

Eye-glass wearers should "roll back" the rubber cups on the rear objectives so they can get closer to them. This will help place your eyes closer to the objectives and allow you to make full use of the optics.

Which brings up an important point: Never purchase a pair of binocs without first looking through the particular model in which you are interested. Many companies have displays at hunting shows and will give you the opportunity to look through their products. They will also have personnel available to answer your questions.

If a hunting partner has a pair of binoculars you are interested in, ask to use his for a day in the field before making a purchase.

Purchase the highest-quality optics you can afford—they are a long-term investment.

Steiner's Whitetail model, an innovative pair of binoculars, has a built-in rangefinder. These enable a hunter to estimate the distance of a whitetail, mule deer or pronghorn antelope within 25 yards.

Owning the very finest binoculars available, however, will do little good if you do not use them. I normally replace the neck strap on my hunting binoculars with a shorter and wider strap—wider so it doesn't cut into my neck when carrying them for long hours and shorter so it's not in the way.

If you are hunting in the brush or happen to see the blink of an eye, the wag of a tail or even the glint of antler or horn, use your binoculars to closely investigate movement. However, make your movements slow and deliberate. Most wild animals notice quick or rapid movement. With my binoculars, I have often spotted deer standing statue-still in the shadows. Had it not been for the binoculars, I would have most likely passed over that "something a little different" from a tree limb.

Binocs also help when "looking through" a leafy screen hiding a deer. You can focus on the animal behind the screen of leaves rather than on the leaves themselves.

Always be thorough when glassing and take full advantage of your binoculars' capabilities. A few years ago, I hunted mule deer in the Colorado mountains with a friend. Each time we glassed an opposite hillside, my friend would simply scan across a huge expanse of rocks, brush and trees. If something was not standing there in full sight, he was ready to declare the area void of deer.

Experience had taught me to sit down, get comfortable, rest my elbows on my knees and spend at least 10 to 20 minutes glassing likely looking spots on the opposite hillsides and slopes. Many times I have decided the slope contained no game only to spot a bedded deer just as I was about to move.

When glassing, find a comfortable place where, if possible, you can lean against a rock or tree. This will help steady your glassing efforts.

Once you are settled in and comfortable, mentally superimpose a grid on the area you want to glass. Thoroughly pick apart each section of the grid after a cursory glass of the area.

This highly successful glassing technique is used by my occasional hunting companion and fellow NAHC Member, Jay Gates of Arizona. Jay quite often uses a tripod to steady his binoculars and help him effectively glass each of the imaginary grids. I normally carry a pair of crossed sticks (shooting sticks) when hunting to help steady my rifle or handgun when shooting; they also double as a rest to help steady my binoculars when glassing. Using a rest to hold the binoculars when I'm comfortably seated makes it much easier for me to stay longer and do a more thorough job of glassing.

Remember that you're not looking for a whole animal. You must search out the odd looking snag that turns into a hind leg, the flutter of a bird's wing that turns into an ear and the discolored limb that turns into an ivory antler tip.

Finally, a pair of high-quality binoculars is an essential piece of safety equipment. Before raising your gun, you must always identify your target with 100 percent accuracy.

For extended glassing sessions, shooting sticks will steady your binoculars and reduce eye fatigue. Shooting sticks also double as a rest to steady a rifle or handgun. When glassing large areas, experienced hunters mentally superimpose a grid on the area.

Rifle Scopes

Hunting was certainly different when I was a child—in the early l950s in the gravel hills just north of Texas' Gulf Coast Prairie. In those days, almost everyone in our rural community of Zimmerscheidt hunted. Even so, very few deer were seen and even fewer were taken.

One of the biggest events in my life, as far as I was concerned, occurred when my dad bought our first rifle scopes—Weaver K4s. To me, that meant our little East Texas farming and ranching community had finally come "of age!"

Rifle scopes had been around for quite a few years. Initially, they were brass tubes with wire sighting devices. The earliest scope reticles were actually "crossed hairs." It wasn't until the l950s that scopes really became popular.

Today, optical sights are so popular that it's difficult to find a hunter who does not have a scope on his rifle or handgun.

Simply put, a rifle scope's greatest advantage is that it places both the target and the sighting reticle on the same focal plane. This phenomenon makes a scope far superior to using open sights in most shooting situations.

When shooting open sights the shooter has to either focus on the sights or the target. That requires having to refocus rapidly from one to the other. A rifle scope eliminates this problem by putting both the reticle (sighting device) and the target in focus at the same time.

The scope's second great advantage is magnification. This makes the target appear larger and easier to see in detail. These attributes, in turn, facilitate precise shot placement.

For example, if a deer is 100 yards distant, it will appear as if only 25 yards away with a 4X (power) scope. Using open or iron sights at the same distance, you would find the majority of the deer would be covered by the notched rear sight and front post. The crosshaired-reticle scope with ½-inch minute of angle covers a ½-inch area at 100 yards. With most modern rifles, the point blank range is essentially 300 yards. An open-sight rifle using a $\frac{1}{10}$-inch front bead covers about 30 inches at 300 yards; the same aforementioned scope reticle covers only 1½ inches.

Today, there are many different scopes available to the hunter, varying considerably in price. There are normal-sized front objectives and large front objectives, varmint scopes and hunting scopes, normal field of view and wide fields, regular-sized and compact-sized, and there are long eye relief scopes (primarily for handguns or for mounting in front of the rifle action for quick pointing).

A rifle scope places both the target and the sighting device on the same focal plane. This is invaluable when in a shooting situation. Most hunters have scopes mounted on their rifles or handguns.

Quite often I see extremely well-made or even custom-made rifles topped with lesser quality optics. Most properly bedded rifles can be extremely accurate with the right ammunition. The weak link to accuracy is often the optics. Hunters should buy the best-quality scopes they can afford.

Magnification is also important. Pertaining to magnification, the hunter has two scope options: fixed power and variable power.

Generally, fixed power scopes are smaller in size, lighter weight, lower priced and have fewer moving parts. Variables, on the other hand, are larger, a bit heavier, higher priced and have more moving parts. Thus, there is a greater opportunity for something to go wrong with a variable.

Although I like to keep things as simple as possible, nearly all my rifle and handgun scopes are variables. Personally, I enjoy and appreciate the ability to "crank up or crank down" the power (actually magnification), depending upon the hunting conditions. For many

Iron Sight vs. Scope

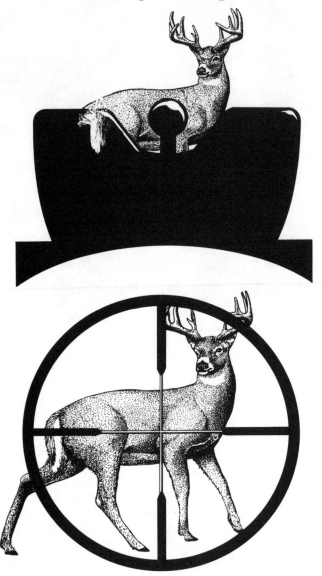

Both of these deer are 100 yards away. With standard iron sights (top), there is no magnification and much of the deer is covered by the notched rear and front post sight. Through a 4X scope (bottom), the deer is four times larger, and the cross hairs cover a ½-inch sliver.

years, I have used the various Leupold variables, as well as the various Simmons scopes, such as the 44 Mag and, more recently, the Whitetail Classics. The most popular scopes in the country seem to be the variables.

There are many advantages to using a variable scope with Duplex cross hairs, such as using it to determine range. By knowing the distance covered between the actual cross of the cross hairs and where the heavier portion of the cross hairs begins, a hunter can easily estimate ranges to beyond 400 yards. If a deer-sized animal standing broadside fits between the thicker portions of my cross hairs (with my Simmons and Leupold scopes) and the scope is set at nearly 8X, the animal is approximately 400 yards distant. Throughout the year, I practice estimating distances using life-sized deer targets. Caution: Don't assume that every scope is the same. The distance covered by the thin, inside cross hairs can vary depending upon the manufacturer and even the scope mode.

There are some scopes with built-in rangefinders; if an animal fits between a certain set of lines, it is a predetermined distance.

Personally, I find several "cross hairs" extremely confusing. In many instances, the "animal of a lifetime" may allow you less than five seconds to see him, evaluate him and execute a shot. In those anxious and excited moments, I don't want to figure out which level of the cross hairs to use!

There are many shapes and sizes of cross hairs, including the Duplex, Multi-X, 4 Plex, Post and more. Most are a matter of personal preference. The broader or heavier cross hairs seem to work better under less-than-ideal light conditions. My choice of the lot, mentioned earlier, is the Duplex type, heavy and then finer where they cross. Keep it simple.

There are several low-light scopes on the market today, including some of the expensive European scopes like Zeiss, Schmidt & Bender, Steiner, Swarovski and possibly others. Several American companies have entered the field, even though most of the scopes are not made in America. Those which I have considerable experience with include the Leupold Vari-X III, 3.5X10-50mm and the Simmons 44 Mag. Other companies include Nikon, Pentax, Nichols, Redfield and their Illuminator series, Tasco, Burris and others. Due to the large front objective lens on the Leupold, the exit pupil is still 5.0mm—even at 10X. (This is determined by dividing the power, in this case 10, into the size of the front objective, 50mm.) These low-light scopes work extremely well early in the morning and late in the afternoon, especially on heavily overcast days. In even the poorest

Using Scope As Rangefinder

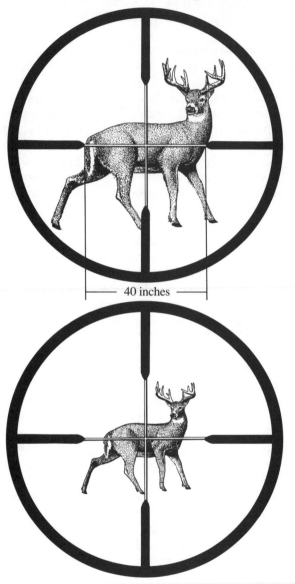

If an average whitetail standing broadside fits between the thicker portions of your 8X scope's cross hairs (top), the deer is 400 yards distant. (An average whitetail is about 40 inches in length.) If the whitetail is smaller than the thin, inside cross hairs (bottom), he is more than 400 yards away.

light conditions, the adult human eye can accept an exit pupil of about 7mm, anything beyond that figure is wasted.

A popular term often heard in conjunction with scopes is "parallax." Parallax is the condition that exists when the image formed by the objective lens does not lie on the same plane as the scope's reticle. Most scope manufacturers preset the "parallax-free distance" at 100 yards. The only time the hunter should consider parallax is if he is a serious varmint or target shooter. It should not be of any concern to the hunter who is after primarily deer-sized and larger game. To me, external parallax adjustments on hunting scopes are unnecessary. They simply confuse things and can cause problems.

Handgun scopes have come a long way. Most of these are LER (Long Eye Relief) or EER (Extended Eye Relief). When the scopes are held about 16 to 25 inches away from the eye, the shooter can still see the full view of the scope. Those which I have used with great success in the past (with such heavy-duty calibers as the .309 JDJ, .45-70 Gov., .375 JDJ and others) include those made by Bausch & Lomb, Burris's new 3X9 LER PLEX, Thompson/Center, Leupold and Simmons 2.5X7.

I also have viewed the Steiner Penetrator. The Penetrator is color-discriminating, meaning it maximizes light transmission in the red part of the spectrum and reflects blue and green light. This in theory enhances the hunter's ability to spot game against a forest background. In "playing" with the scope, I had an opportunity to check it out. The Steiner Penetrator does help pick out reds and browns from the background of greens and blues. However, this brings up an interesting point: Never, under any circumstances, use your rifle scope as you would binoculars or a spotting scope.

While hunting public land in the West, I have glassed with binoculars only to spot a distant hunter looking at me through his rifle scope! In talking with several NAHC Shooting Advisory Council members and staff writers, I've learned that this subject has frequently come up. One senior writer said, "Anytime I see someone looking at me through a rifle scope I can only assume he has intentions of shooting me. I'll take whatever steps necessary to prevent this." Please never use your rifle scope to "scope out" what might be a fellow hunter!

There are various scopes on the market today to choose from. For years, the high-gloss finishes were the norm. These shiny finishes were nice to look at, but they revealed a hunter's presence. Thankfully, some companies began using satin and matte finishes on their scopes' exteriors. I think the matte finish on my various Leupolds

With new technology, handgun scopes have become more and more valuable to handgun hunters. Most are LER (Long Eye Relief) or EER (Extended Eye Relief); when the scope is held 16 to 25 inches from the eye, the hunter still sees the scope's full view.

help in reducing the glare and shine seen by animals from a distance. Simmons has taken scope finishes one step further with their non-glare BlackGranite finish.

If hunting in wet weather, do not let water sit for any length of time in the lens cup.

If you will be hunting in cold weather, leave your rifle safely stored outside instead of inside where the temperature is considerably warmer. This helps prevent outside fogging of the lenses. Who knows, the "buck of a lifetime" might be within 200 yards of camp. It would be terrible to miss such an opportunity because the outside of your scope lenses are fogged.

Also, to get the most from your hunting optics you must keep them clean. First, use scope lens covers. Some type of lens covers is normally provided when you purchase a scope, but specialized, after-market models are produced by Michael's of Oregon, Butler Creek and others. Most after-market scope covers feature quick-release mechanisms which, in many situations, allow you to keep the covers in place until the moment of truth. The lens covers should be kept in place until you are preparing to shoot, particularly in inclement weather and when you're carrying a rifle in a scabbard while riding an ATV or on horseback.

Some manufacturers, like Swarovski, offer their scopes with "see-through" lens covers. In rain and snow, you can keep these transparent protectors in place and yet aim through them if a surprise shot arises.

Eventually, your scope lenses will need cleaning. Generally, this should be done at home or at least in camp where you have some control over airborne dust, moisture and temperature. However, if you need to clean your scope in the field, be sure to carry the materials to do the job correctly; improper cleaning can permanently impair the quality of even the finest hunting optics!

The well-equipped lens-cleaning kit should include a retractable mohair brush, cotton swabs, lens paper patches, lens cleaning solution, canned air and a pad of full-sized lens paper. These items can be purchased at your local camera store.

The first step in cleaning your scope lenses is to be certain they are free of dust and dirt particles. Spray the lenses with canned air or gently brush them with a mohair brush. Be sure to remove any particles stuck around the edge of the lenses, too.

The optical coatings which make scopes bright and clear are delicate. They can be permanently scratched by grinding dust particles against them.

Only after all visible dirt particles are gone should you put one or two drops of cleaning solution on the lens. Then, using a gentle circular motion, clean the lens with lens paper.

You should never use a paper towel or any wood-fiber product to clean coated optics. Avoid using your handkerchief, too. If you'll be using your hunting optics in a dusty environment, treat the lenses with an anti-static liquid.

A scope does a lot for a hunter. It makes his sport considerably safer, more productive and more enjoyable. Wisely select a scope and it will become more than just a tool. It will become a trusted old friend.

Spotting Scopes

Years ago, the only use most hunters had for spotting scopes was when sighting in a rifle on the range or hunting pronghorn in the West. Today, NAHC Members in the Northeast, Southeast and Midwest are discovering a passle of new uses for modern spotting scopes. The reason? Land practices and farming techniques have changed. Where there were once dense forests, there are now scattered fields and meadows. Powerline and utility rights-of-way cut through dense thickets and forests. And large grain fields stretch out for hundreds of yards. Serious hunters have discovered that a spotting scope is a valuable and versatile piece of equipment.

This is especially true for hunters who pursue trophy-quality animals. There is no better way to evaluate a trophy animal than bringing him up close.

My first spotting scope was purchased quite a few years ago. It was a 20X Bushnell Sentry II. Today, it is mounted on a discarded rifle stock and serves as my ''rough piece''—it takes a beating during preseason scouting trips.

This particular model was one of the first affordable spotting scopes that was not too heavy or too bulky. During the past several years, many new spotting scopes which are considerably smaller and significantly lighter have been introduced.

In selecting a spotting scope for hunting, there are several factors to consider. Always take the time to look through the spotting scopes you are considering and learn each model's strengths and weaknesses. Get outside with them so you're not judging optical quality through cheap window glass.

The exit-pupil principles that apply to binoculars also apply to spotting scopes. If you wear eyeglasses or will be wearing sunglasses while hunting, consider this before making a purchase. A spotting

The popularity of spotting scopes has dramatically increased in recent years. Most hunters pursuing trophy-quality animals think that spotting scopes are necessary because they bring the animal up close. Most spotting scopes are monocular; therefore, they cause eye strain and fatigue when used for long periods of time.

scope is a major investment. Be sure it "fits" your personal and hunting needs before spending the money.

When hunting, it is usually a good idea to first locate game with binoculars, then switch to the higher-powered spotting scope to get a closer look at the subject. Thus, to some extent, "field of view" is important. However, the "area of view" is also important. For instance, with 7X binoculars the field of view at 1,000 yards is 375 feet, while the area of view at 1,000 yards is 12,272 square yards. With a 21X spotting scope, the field of view at 1,000 yards is 125 feet, while the area of view at the same distance is 1,364 square yards.

With a 42X spotting scope, the field of view is 62.5 feet at 1,000 yards, while the area of view is 341 square yards (or essentially, an area of 15 yards by 20 yards). These limitations become extremely important when glassing distant game. Think of the tedious job it would be to thoroughly glass a distant hillside 341 square yards at a time! Using a 42X spotting scope, you would spend 40 hours covering the same area you could cover in one hour with 7X binoculars.

This, then, is the primary reason not to use the spotting scope to spot game, even though the name implies such a scope would be used for spotting. A better monicker might be a "study" scope.

Because most spotting scopes are monocular, they are not intended to be looked through for any length of time without causing eye strain and fatigue.

The alternative to the monocular spotting scope is high-magnification binoculars, such as Bausch & Lomb's Terrestrial Binocular (20X80), Steiner's 15X80 and Zeiss' 15X60 and 20X60.

These binoculars allow you to take advantage of better vision through both eyes and to bring an animal "close up." Because it is natural for us to see with both eyes open, extended viewing through binoculars is more comfortable than through a spotting scope.

Although large-magnification, high-quality binoculars are, for the most part, bulkier and more expensive than spotting scopes of similar power and quality, they are the choice of many guides and hunters. Anyone who spends hundreds of hours per year glassing for animals will certainly appreciate the difference. (Because the high magnification exaggerates hand movement, these binoculars must be used from a tripod.)

Carl Zeiss Optical introduced to the American market specially designed 20X binoculars which can be hand-held—the Zeiss 20X60 S. (The "S" stands for stabilized.) The all-new technology of these Zeiss binoculars is relatively compact, not much larger or heavier

High magnification binoculars offer a comfortable alternative to monocular spotting scopes. Steiner high-magnification binoculars are among the most popular with hunters who spend a lot of time seriously glassing for trophy big game.

than other high-magnification binocular rigs. Unfortunately, this kind of technology and quality is not inexpensive. The suggested retail price is more than $4,000 and availability is limited.

Excellent models of traditional, tripod-bound, high-magnification binoculars can be purchased at more reasonable prices.

With spotting scopes, there are two basic options: fixed power and variable power (zooms). Personally, I prefer the fixed power with no greater than 20- to 25-power magnifications, such as Leupold's 20X50 Rubber Armored, Burris' ''The Spotter'' 20X50, and Simmons' compact 25X50 Model 1206. These, even with a tripod, are rather lightweight and easily fit inside a day pack or a large fanny pack. Nikon's 20X60 Gray Rubber Armored model is a bit heavier and larger; however, it is an excellent fixed-power spotting scope.

In fixed powers, the 20- to 25-power scopes are ideal; however, the 30X should be the upper limit. Even though the image continues to get larger above 30X, the resolution, or sharpness, of the image does not. Another problem I have encountered with spotting scopes over 30X is mirage. This becomes especially true when hunting in the Southwest, and, to some extent, when hunting in the higher mountains during warm weather.

Some hunters, however, prefer to use zoom or variable-power spotting scopes. They do provide the option to switch powers, depending upon hunting conditions and the weather. Some popular zoom spotting scopes include Simmons 17-52X Model 1212, Redfield 18-42X Regal II, Bushnell 15-45X Spacemaster, Jason 15-45X Model 344, Bausch & Lomb 15-45X Elite and Swarovski 25-40X.

In most hunting conditions and situations where a spotting scope is used, both weight and size become critical factors. Perhaps that is why I prefer fixed-power scopes. In most instances, even with a sturdy, lightweight tripod, those fixed-power spotting scopes weigh less than 3 pounds. Some brightness and resolution may be lost by not using a 70mm or larger objective lens, but the 50mms will do a fine job. I will gladly make that nominal sacrifice for the reduction in weight.

There are many different kinds and styles of spotting scopes. Given the option, I would select a rubber-armored scope. These seem to take more accidental punishment and resist scratches and dents. These also have a dull finish which does not reveal my presence to a sharp-eyed animal hundreds of yards away.

Use binoculars to spot game, then switch to the spotting scope to further evaluate the animal. Be reminded that finding the game through the larger magnification but narrower field-of-view optic is often difficult unless you're using a spotting scope equipped with a sighting device. This is usually a low-powered (1-3X) finder scope that is attached to the more powerful scope. Placing the area you want to evaluate in the center of the sighting device should then put it within the higher magnification scope's field of view.

A spotting scope is only as good as its rest. If I don't have a solid rest for my scope, I would rather use my binoculars. If you invest in a spotting scope or pair of binoculars of more than 10X, you will need a sturdy, well-built tripod.

A good second investment is a window mount. These work extremely well when scouting from a vehicle or permanent hunting blind. Anything you can do to steady the spotting scope will make it easier to use. You can also attach it to a discarded rifle stock which makes for a solid, yet quickly mobile rest.

If your spotting scope does not come with a protective case, buy

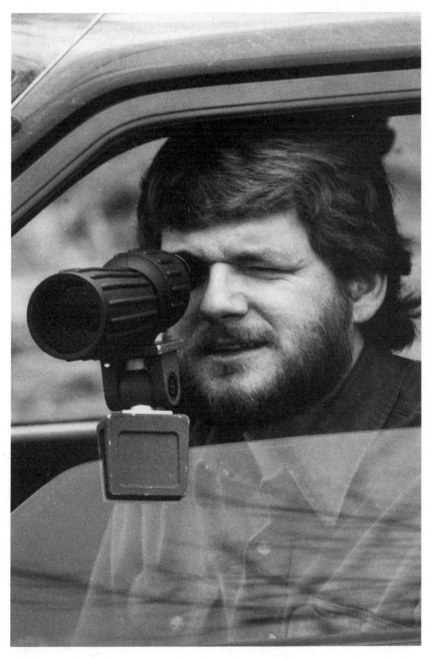

Window mounts work well when spotting from a vehicle. They also are great when attached to permanent blinds. Steadying your scope should be a No. 1 priority.

one. The lenses can easily become scratched if not protected. When the scope is not in use, its lenses should be properly covered. Keep the lenses free of dust whenever possible.

To get the most out of your spotting scope, select one which suits you and your purpose. More magnification is not always better. Always use a tripod whenever possible. If you do not use a tripod, use a window mount, a tree fork or a folded up jacket on top of a rock.

Practice using the spotting scope and tripod. This also includes learning how to use and adjust the focus. I have seen spotting-scope users get completely disenchanted because each time they adjusted the focus the entire scope moved. A hunting trip is not a good time to experiment and learn how to use your spotting scope!

3

Taking That First Whitetail
by Kevin Howard

Visually, the deer blind looks like a big, round hay bale. However, my 6-year-old son, Andrew, and 9-year-old daughter, Erin, refer to their blind as "The Huntin' Hut." The blind was a Christmas gift from my good friend and hunting partner, Frank Mackey. He originally built it for bowhunting; however, I introduced my children to deer hunting with it.

Almost every person in North America has the opportunity to hunt deer. White-tailed deer populations have been exploding across the country and mule-deer herds are increasing in most Western states. There has never been a better time to learn how to hunt deer.

When I was growing up, there were few deer in our part of Missouri. If we saw one on our farm, it was the talk of the town. When I became a junior in high school, the deer population had grown substantially, and more people thought about hunting them. Although some hunters were successful, most lacked deer hunting skills.

I was fortunate enough to have a teacher who hunted in other parts of the state where the deer population had returned to considerable numbers. Mr. Kraus has been gone for many years, but my memories of him and my first deer are vivid.

An immigrant from Austria, Mr. Kraus owned a successful road construction business in St. Louis. My father let him hunt on our land. That decision eventually led to a friendship that spanned more than 20 years.

Mr. Kraus hunted rabbits and squirrels on our farm, but always went to the Missouri Ozarks each fall to hunt deer. When we started seeing deer on our land, Mr. Kraus introduced my brother and me to deer hunting.

Squirrel season in Missouri runs from late May through December. Mr. Kraus always combined his squirrel hunts with scouting trips for deer. He showed me how to find deer trails, where deer bedded, what they ate and how to set up stands to catch them moving from one area to another.

It was Mr. Kraus who helped me take my first deer in the fall of my senior year of high school. Although I've taken a number of larger deer since then, the six-point buck I killed while hunting with Mr. Kraus will always be one of my most memorable trophies.

Mr. Kraus and I had decided that this was going to be the year I took my first deer. Before the season opened, we spent several weekends scouting, checking sign and watching for deer. By the season's opening day in mid-November, we had chosen both a morning and evening stand.

The first morning of the season my brother killed an 11-point buck from an oak ridge above our house. It was the biggest deer we had ever seen! I'll admit I was jealous; Mr. Kraus and I worked hard scouting deer all fall while my brother had been at college. But Mr. Kraus and I weren't worried. We had an evening stand in the river bottom where we had seen deer come out and feed every night for almost a week.

About noon on that opening Saturday, I started feeling bad. By 1 p.m. I had a bad case of the flu. Mr. Kraus really wanted me to get a deer, and he felt almost as bad as I did because I couldn't hunt.

The flu lasted through Sunday. By the time I felt like hunting, it was Monday morning. My hunting time was going to be shortened because of school. Mr. Kraus took off work and hunted with me every morning and evening. We would hunt as late as possible each morning and then I would take off for school.

On Thursday morning, our persistence paid off. Mr. Kraus had found a well-worn deer path that crossed a creek which ran between a small patch of woods and a big cornfield. Mr. Kraus had chosen a spot to set up a ground blind on the top of one of the high banks. About 7 a.m., we saw a buck jump over the levy on the creek's opposite side. Something must have spooked the buck because he was running almost full speed. He bounded along the edge of the far side of the creek. When he was directly across from us, I shot.

The buck didn't even break stride as he went up over the opposite

Children love to be part of the hunting world, and many are learning to hunt at rather young ages. This youngster (Andrew Howard) dreams of the day he can take a deer like his father's.

bank. Before he reached the top, I jacked another shell into my bolt-action gun and tried desperately to put the sights on the middle of his back. The deer was coming down from one of his jumps when I pulled the trigger. Instead of hitting him in the back, the bullet went through the side of his head. He dropped instantly.

Mr. Kraus and I yelled and did a dance. We field dressed the deer and got back to the house in time for school. Mr. Kraus ended his deer hunting season that day. His season's success was me taking my first deer. I will never forget his unselfish determination in helping me get that deer. Each time I look at my mounted six-pointer, I think of a long-ago Thursday morning when I got my first deer.

The first, and maybe the most important, lesson to teach a young hunter is respect and love for nature and the deer. Teaching youngsters about nature and hunting can begin before they are a year old. My wife and I began reading to our children when they were only a few months old. In addition to the varied children's books available, we incorporated conservation magazines and outdoor material. By the time they were three years old, both had been exposed to many of my hunting publications and understood the basics of hunting and the role it plays in wildlife conservation.

I must warn you about some of the so-called conservation materials for children, however. Some magazines have false information on such things as game populations and the role hunting plays in wildlife management. You should screen anything you want to share with your children.

With a knowledge and respect of nature and game animals, a young hunter will appreciate this ongoing life cycle. Give them a good start and they will develop into ethical, responsible hunters.

By the time my children were five years old, they could find deer tracks, rubs, scrapes and trails. It has almost become a contest to see who can spot a deer or sign first.

Scouting trips introduce young or new hunters to deer hunting. In the spring, you can combine mushroom hunting with checking buck signs remaining from the previous fall's rut. Walking through prime spots in the spring gives you a chance to show the young hunter the type of sign to look for. By doing this, you won't disturb your hunting area for the fall and you may find the sign of a real trophy.

Late summer is a great time to determine the buck population in your hunting area. My family drives in the late afternoon and evening this time of year. We often see deer around the edges of fields or near water. The bucks seem more relaxed, and, though they still have velvet on their racks, you can see each deer's potential.

It is important to teach children to respect nature and animals. Various reading material is available; however, be careful when selecting it. Also, children should be taught scouting techniques, such as finding sign, before learning how to shoot a rifle.

Most states require hunters to attend a hunting education class. These classes are about 10 hours long and cover the following subjects: equipment (gun and bow) safety, conservation, ethics, game laws and landowner respect.

Spotting and observing deer with a good pair of optics is excellent training for young hunters. This allows them to catch the movements and actions of deer before the hunting season opens.

Preparing For The Hunt

In all but a few states, a mandatory requirement for purchasing a hunting license is attending a class on hunter education. The basic hunter education course is 10 hours long and covers many subjects. In addition to the basic gun safety section, hunter education courses teach conservation, ethics, game laws and landowner respect. Their mission is to produce responsible, ethical hunters for today and the future.

Learning To Shoot

Recreational shooting is fun and a good way to teach responsibility, respect and self-discipline. Like other aspects of deer hunting, people can learn how to use a gun at a young age.

My children shot air guns, under close supervision, when they were five years old. Today's air guns come with safeties, good sights and fair trigger pulls. They are also extremely accurate. Air guns help teach sight pictures and trigger control.

Once a young shooter masters the air gun, a .22 rifle is the next step. With a .22 you can stretch the shooting distance to 50, 75 or even 100 yards. Most .22s are grooved for scope mounts and can accommodate a full-sized scope. I put the duplex-type reticle scopes I use on my deer rifles on my .22s. That way, I can practice using the same sight picture I have with a big-bore gun. It is also great practice for the young hunter.

Once the young shooter has begun to master the .22, it's time to move them up to a centerfire rifle. A varmit-caliber gun works best. A rifle in .22-250 or .223 gives the shooter a feel for a bigger gun, but with less recoil. However, these guns will probably be a little too big for the youngster.

If the young hunter is going to become a proficient shooter, he must have a gun that fits. Trying to teach someone to shoot with a gun that is too big is discouraging. Purchase a gun that the shooter can handle instead of starting them on a hand-me-down.

When it's time to choose the young hunter's first deer rifle, a couple of things should be considered. First of all, you need to choose a caliber that produces sufficient energy to kill the game you're hunting. Calibers that have sufficient power to take deer, yet have recoil that is manageable by a smaller person, include the .243 Win., 6mm Rem., .30-30 Win., 7mm-08 Rem. and .308 Win. These calibers come in various gun types.

The rifle action you choose is really a matter of preference. A bolt-action rifle is hard to beat; they are accurate and dependable. One of the new lightweight models with either a wood or synthetic stock would be an excellent choice. Single-shot models are also dependable and accurate; however, they don't give the option of a quick follow-up shot.

Lever-action guns are lightweight, quick-handling and available in many calibers. However, it can be difficult for the young hunter to execute a follow-up shot with a lever-type gun.

The semi-automatics and the pump rifles can also be considered. These can match the type of shotgun a young shooter is using. Both actions come in several calibers.

Several guns will meet the needs of a young hunter. Winchester and Browning have both bolt-action and lever-action guns that make excellent choices for the first deer rifle. Browning also offers single-shot and semi-automatic action guns. Remington has bolt-action, semi-automatic and pump guns in various calibers. Ruger has both single-shot and bolt-action guns. And Marlin offers lever-action guns in various calibers.

Learning to shoot at an early age is becoming more and more common in hunting families. Usually the youngster starts with an air gun and eventually moves to the .22 rifle. Once the .22 is mastered, the centerfire rifle is next. The final step is the youngster's first deer rifle, which should be selected carefully.

Several states require using shotguns and slugs during their firearms deer season. If you hunt in one of these states, it's just as important to teach good shooting skills to your new hunter. There have been dramatic improvements in shotgun equipment and ammunition for deer hunting.

The 12-gauge is undoubtedly the most popular shotgun for deer hunting. The 12-gauge, however, kicks like a mule, even if it's a semi-automatic gun. A better choice for a young hunter would be a 20-gauge.

Rifle slugs in a 20-gauge still weigh ¾ ounce. That's a big hunk of lead traveling at almost 1,600 feet per second. In the sabot-type slug, the 20-gauge projectile weighs ⅝ ounce and, when combined with a rifled barrel and scope, makes an excellent shotgun combination for deer. Some type of adjustable sighting system on the shotgun is needed. I prefer a scope, but good iron sights are also available. A shotgun must be sighted in just like a rifle. To do this, you need adjustable sights.

Continue sighting in the new gun and shooting from a bench until the youngster builds confidence and shooting skills to a satisfactory level. Once the new hunter masters skills in shooting proper groups from the bench, he should practice from sitting and kneeling positions. He should also shoot from a standing position using a tree, rock or some other object for support. I would suggest shooting some in an off-hand standing position, too. It is difficult to hit your target from this position; it should only be used as a last resort.

It is also important to shoot at life-sized deer targets. This allows the shooter to see what the sight picture will look like on the real thing. Practicing in an area similar to the terrain you will be hunting also will benefit the new hunter. Placing deer targets at various ranges among trees and bushes helps prepare the hunter even more.

Another good exercise is taking outdoor magazines like *North American Hunter* and aiming at photographs of deer appearing in the magazine. (Of course, it's important to make sure the gun is not loaded. For extra safety, I leave the action of the gun open.) These photos show deer in natural surroundings and at various angles. A fun game to play is "shoot or don't shoot." Have the youngster look at a photo and quickly tell you if he has a good shot at the deer and where he would aim.

The best time to introduce a young person to deer hunting is during rifle season. However, many states offer bow-and-arrow hunting, and several states also have special muzzleloader seasons.

Bows And Muzzleloaders

If a person hunts with a bow or black-powder gun, he must become very proficient with the equipment. Most experts feel a bow should have at least a 45-pound draw, with 50 pounds being even better, for deer-sized animals. Be sure your young hunter can handle a bow of this weight if he is going to hunt deer with it.

There have been tremendous improvements in black-powder guns. The new generation of muzzleloaders shoot almost as accurately as big-bore rifles. The only problem is you only have one shot.

Keep in mind that when young people begin deer hunting, they must be proficient with the type of weapon they are using. This teaches responsibility and respect for weapons and the game that they will hunt.

When And Where To Hunt

Opening day of deer season is like a holiday in many states. Hundreds of thousands of deer hunters head for the woods to partake in the hunting tradition. Introducing a young hunter to deer hunting should be done on another day of the season.

Several states have enacted special "youth" deer seasons. Some states actually have separate seasons for youth; others have special area hunts. These special events introduce new people to the sport under a more controlled atmosphere.

Many states enact antlerless-only deer hunts to reduce doe populations. If these types of hunts are available in your state, they are a great way to help young hunters take their first deer. It seems the woods and fields are less crowded. This makes it easier to focus on the hunt. The hunts usually require the accompaniment of a non-hunting adult.

Helping manage deer herds is another way to find a hunting area for a young hunter. In some states, the rising deer population has become a big problem. To maintain a healthy population, deer numbers must be kept at a level compatible with the habitat. There is nothing wrong with a young hunter taking a doe as his first deer. In some cases, it is the best thing for the herd.

State conservation departments also can help you locate good hunting areas. There may be landowners who have problems with crop damage from an overpopulation of deer. If you can find a landowner who needs deer harvested on his land, it is a lot easier to get permission to hunt. Go to the landowner well before the season starts and take your young hunter with you. Explain to the owner that you are looking for a place for your youngster's first deer hunt. Tell him you are willing to take only does and you won't hunt yourself. If you approach a landowner in this way, he will most likely be receptive to letting you hunt his land. (Be sure that one of the lessons you teach your new hunter is respect for landowners and their property.)

Youths who may not have relatives or friends to teach them how to hunt deer can learn from concerned volunteers through programs such as Operation Orphans in Mason, Texas.

The Operation Orphans program began in 1960 when Gene Asby, a conservation officer in Texas, recognized the need to reduce the deer population on several ranches. At the same time, he wanted to give youths who might not otherwise have the chance to hunt an opportunity to experience the sport.

The solution was to take youth from orphanages, team them with a volunteer guide and put them on a ranch that needed to reduce its doe population. According to hunt coordinator Mike Dall, almost 600 youngsters hunt each year during one of the four special white-tailed deer hunts or the exotic animal hunt.

Anywhere from 75 to 100 ranchers open their land to the special orphan hunt. As many as 200 different volunteers help guide the young people. Texas has a huge deer population which needs to be reduced annually. The increase in deer population throughout the

Operation Orphans in Mason, Texas, offers children the chance to experience the joy of hunting. Over 200 volunteers guide and teach these youngsters. This program helps control the deer population on various Texas ranches.

country may warrant a program like this in other states. These programs are simply a win-win situation: New people are introduced to the sport and several deer herds are kept under control.

The Hunt

In the fall, it's time to get serious about where you and your young hunter will hunt. Scouting trips help locate the best areas and the right place to set up a stand. Because excitement and deer hunting go hand in hand, I think it is best to hunt from a fixed position. Stand-hunting allows both of you to sit together, and enables the older hunter to coach the youngster throughout the hunt.

When located downwind of a deer trail, a ground blind works great. Ground blinds are safe and almost essential if you are hunting with a young person.

The "Huntin' Hut" (mentioned earlier in this chapter) is one of the best ground blinds. This big, round hay-bale imitation was the

Operation Orphans is just one program that gives orphans the opportunity to hunt. The pride that comes with taking a white-tailed deer for the first time is unforgettable. All children should have the chance to experience it.

idea of a friend whose 6-year-old boy wanted to hunt with him. Because most of the hay in his area was put up in these big bales, deer are around them all the time. It's the perfect camouflage.

To make the bale blind, two 4x4s, about 7 feet long, are laid out for runners. Two 6-foot-long 2x6s are nailed on top of the ends of the 4x4s. This gives a 6- by 7-foot base. Then a concrete reinforcement wire is attached to the top of one of the 4x4s; it is bent in the round shape of a bale over to the other 4x4. The top center of the wire is about 5 feet high. The bale blind's basic structure is completed with the wire. The ends of the bale are flat, making it look like a wire-mesh big bale. Shooting ports are cut in the wire and plywood doors are installed on both sides and on one end. The holes are about 1-foot square. A door for entering the blind, 2 feet square, is cut in the other end of the bale. The wire frame is then covered with black plastic. Another layer of wire is cut to go over the bale with enough room for a 3-inch layer of hay left between the wire and plastic.

When finished, the bale blind is almost airtight. By opening one shooting port at a time, very little light gets into the blind and deer that are 15 yards away cannot see inside.

In the fall, I put the blind at the crossing of two well-used deer trails within easy walking distance of where we park our truck. My son and daughter take turns going with me to hunt in the blind. Because they can move around without spooking deer, they tend to stay out longer. I think it's too difficult for children to sit still for any length of time. This way, they can expend a certain amount of energy, which provides them with a little more patience. They have seen deer, turkey, squirrels, rabbits, raccoons, opossums, owls and other wildlife from the blind. I've been amazed at how little attention deer and other animals pay to the blind. It's been a lot fun for all of us.

Another type of blind that works well for young hunters is a permanent tree stand big enough for two people. In some parts of the country these blinds are like small houses. The added height makes

One of the best camouflage tactics when hunting with young children is the "hunting hut." It allows children to move around without spooking deer and other animals.

observing game easier and helps keep your scent above sensitive noses. Make sure you have a shooting rail around the elevated blind and use safety belts.

The most important thing about any blind is that it lets the young hunter get ready for the shot. Moving without being detected by deer is a big advantage. It gives the hunter extra time to move into a good shooting position.

I still like to sit and admire the animal I've taken. Make sure the successful young hunter takes time to reflect on the part they play in the ongoing process of life and death. Then help them field dress the deer and prepare it for the freezer.

4

Field-Judging Trophy Deer
by Chuck Adams

What constitutes a trophy deer? Some hunters like the challenge, others the taste of the meat. And, of course, there are the hunters who want the world-record rack. This chapter highlights field-judging various deer, including white-tailed, mule, Coues', Columbia black-tailed, Sitka black-tailed and the non-typicals.

The standards set by the two best-known, world-record "trophy" organizations, the Boone and Crockett Club and the Pope and Young Club, are outlined specifically, but the information applies as well for muzzleloader and handgun hunters.

Now you can learn not only what to look for, but where to look.

White-Tailed Deer

The white-tailed deer is every man's big-game animal. More whitetails are harvested in North America than any other species, and populations continue to rise from the Pacific to the Atlantic coastlines. White-tailed deer are hunted in 47 of the 50 states in the United States, plus every province in Canada and most parts of Mexico. If you wish to hunt whitetails, you can travel far or you can stay very close to home.

From a trophy standpoint, however, certain areas are clearly superior to others. Many sportsmen dream about bagging a wall-hanger white-tailed buck, yet continue to hunt year after year in non-trophy locales. Some places, like parts of Pennsylvania, Michigan and Texas, are heavily hunted and nearly devoid of bucks over 3½ years old. Consequently, large-racked trophies are scarce. Other habitats, like the Florida Keys and Anticosti Island, apparently lack the genetic potential or proper forage to produce bucks with "giant" antlers.

Impressive white-tailed bucks still are harvested in many places, but you must do your homework to find likely areas blessed with proper feed, genetics and good trophy management. Some places, like south Texas, Alberta, Saskatchewan, northwestern Montana, Minnesota, Kansas and Wisconsin, are genuine hotspots for giant racks. Others, like New York, Maine, Georgia and Illinois produce nice bucks in only specific locales offering a combination of light hunting pressure, good nutrition and time-tested genetics.

If you want a big buck, don't spin your wheels where forkhorns and small eight-pointers are the rule. Go where the big boys live!

There are more than 30 subspecies of whitetails on the continent. These vary in physical stature from the 80-pound Florida Keys deer to northern whitetails weighing more than 300 pounds.

Nonetheless, all whitetails have certain distinctive traits in common. In the fall, their faces and brows are uniformly brown-gray except for a white band behind the nose and white circles around the eyes. Ears are relatively short compared to body size, averaging 18 inches from tip to tip.

The tail is equally distinctive—a long, fluffy appendage with a topside of gray-brown and an underside of stark white. When it's running, a whitetail usually will lift this "flag" and wag it back and forth—a white signal issued by no other deer. In Western and Midwestern states where whitetails and mule deer may be hunted concurrently, these physical traits set the whitetail apart.

The average whitetail's antlers are also unique, although nontypical racks can defy ready identification. Main beams sprout from the head, curve upward and backward at first, then jut dramatically forward above the nose. White-tailed racks do not normally bifurcate (divide into two branches) like those on blacktails and mule deer. Instead, all tines rise from a common main beam like candles in a row. Also, eyeguards tend to be longer than those on other species of deer.

An average, mature white-tailed buck 4½ to 6½ years old carries a total of 10 typical tines—one eyeguard, one main beam and three upright points per side. Such a deer is called a 10-pointer. A few bucks never progress beyond four points per side, and such eight-pointers can be immense at middle age. A nice non-record, 10-point white-tailed rack will spread to the eartips when viewed from the front. From the side, main beams will project to the back of the nose.

White-tailed deer are by far the most popular game species among hunters. These deer can be found in almost every area of the country; however, finding trophy white-tailed deer is another story.

Record-Book Whitetail

To get into the record books, a typical white-tailed buck must carry a massive rack with extra-long beams (24 to 30 inches long and extending beyond the nose when viewed from the side) and a colossal spread. Main beams should be 4 to 6 inches in base circumference, and antlers should extend 1 to 5 inches beyond each eartip.

Eyeguards will vary between 3 and 8 inches in length; other points will measure 4 to 10 inches. Mass will not be eye-stopping compared to length of beams. Such a buck will carry main beams of 19 to 23 inches in length. Antler bases will measure between 3½ and 4 inches in circumference. A deer of this caliber will score between 120 and 150 B&C points—a definite cut above the norm. Such bucks will also exceed the P&Y bowhunting minimum of 125.

A genuine B&C whitetail is distinctive. To exceed the present minimum record-book score of 170, a buck must carry a massive rack with extra-long beams and a colossal spread. Main beams will measure 24 to 30 inches long and extend beyond the tip of the nose when viewed from the side. Antler mass will be substantial, with main beams measuring 4 to 6 inches in circumference at the base. Antlers will spread 1 to 5 inches beyond each eartip, and primary tines will rise high above the head.

Two typical whitetails in the B&C list have inside main beam spreads of more than 30 inches, but a 23-inch inside spread is par for the course with record-book contenders. Tines will commonly measure 10 or 12 inches in length. Eyeguards can be quite long, too, sometimes exceeding 12 inches on each side. Many typical B&C bucks carry more than three upright tines forward of the eyeguards, increasing the total number of tines to 12 or more. Such racks should be symmetrical with no major non-typical drop tines, "cheaters" jutting to one side, multiple eyeguards, or similar gingerbread. Few hunters will pass up a giant whitetail with non-typical tines, but such a deer can miss B&C as a direct result.

Any typical whitetail scoring over 150 B&C points is impressive on the hoof. To an experienced eye, antlers seem to overpower the animal's head at a glance. Rack coloration can be a bit of a fooler, with light-colored antlers appearing larger in dimension yet less massive than they really are. Dark-brown racks tend to appear more massive and smaller in dimension. Only close scrutiny can help you overcome these size-judging pitfalls.

In-depth research shows that most whitetails in the B&C list were bagged during the peak rutting period between mid-November and mid-December. A whitetail is one of North America's most skittish creatures, and a mature hatrack buck can be almost impossible to locate before he drops his guard to rut. Modern rut-hunting technology, including use of scents, grunt calls and rattling antlers, can give serious hunters a primary edge at this magic time of year.

In addition, time-tested tactics like snow tracking, deer driving and stand-hunting along feeding fields can work well when foliage, hunting pressure and weather are conducive to such ploys.

Mule Deer

Mule deer inhabit 17 Western states plus southwestern Canada and northern Mexico. This magnificent animal sports the largest headgear of the five officially recognized North American deer—a rack commonly spreading beyond 2 feet in width and sprouting four or five points per side.

Any mature mule deer looks huge to the average white-tailed buff. The Colorado game department recently studied antler growth and concluded that 12 percent of 1½-year-old mulie bucks already carried a full four points per side, not counting eyeguards! By age 3½, most typical mule deer sport 4x4 racks plus stubby eyeguards above the brow. Spreads average 20 to 24 inches.

Most first-time Western mule-deer hunters are satisfied with mature, representative bucks. Fortunately, such deer are easy to recognize on the hoof. First of all, animals should carry at least four primary points per side, not counting eyeguards. These should branch like double slingshots from the main beam. Each of the four points should be at least 5 inches. Small fringe points commonly adorn mule-deer antlers, and such gingerbread can be visually desirable. However, make sure your dream buck has four or more major points on each side.

Mule deer—even trophy bucks—sometimes display short eyeguards or lack them entirely. Eyeguards on mule deer seldom grow beyond 4 or 5 inches in length.

How mule deer points are counted varies considerably. In the Midwest and Montana, for example, a 4x4 buck with eyeguards is usually dubbed a five-pointer. Farther south and west, hunters tend to ignore the eyeguards and call such a deer a four-pointer. Southwestern terminology is used by most states offering "early season" or "high-country" trophy-buck hunts. When regulations say "four-point deer or better," they mean a typical mature deer with four primary, bifurcated points per side. Eyeguards do not count.

In eastern-fringe mule-deer states, like Oklahoma, hunters are prone to adopt the white-tailed deer hunter's habit of calling a 4x4 mule deer with eyeguards a 10-pointer. To avoid confusion, check out such regional variations.

What kind of antler dimensions are on a typical mule-deer trophy? The outside of the rack should spread at least to the eartips when ears are cupped alertly forward. Mature bucks measure 20 to 22 inches between the eartips, and any deer with a narrower rack is substandard trophy material. Ideally, your chosen buck's antlers will spread slightly beyond the eartips for a 24- to 26-inch outside spread.

Other visual clues can be helpful in judging trophies. An average buck measures 18 to 20 inches from backline to brisket, letting you judge spread if the animal's ears are deformed or held backward in a relaxed position. Similarly, a healthy buck will measure 18 to 20 inches across the paunch when facing directly toward you or away. If his rack spreads as wide as his body, he's got the width.

Antler mass is difficult to estimate, and won't be a major concern if you're after an average trophy-class deer. Most mule deer do not shed their velvet before early to mid-September, so racks seen on August bowhunts and high-country rifle or muzzleloader hunts appear more massive than they actually are. On autumn deer, amber-colored racks appear more spindly than identical antlers of deep brown. Mulie racks vary considerably in coloration which makes mass comparisons doubly difficult.

Mule deer are quite massive compared to white-tailed deer. They carry the largest head-gear of all five officially recognized North American deer. An average mulie measures 18 to 20 inches from backline to brisket.

Dead-serious mule-deer buffs sometimes set their sights on animals of record-book or near-record-book size. This task requires more ticklish trophy evaluation.

The standard antler-scoring system used by B&C and P&Y places a premium on greatest inside spread of main (forward-most) beams, length of all typical points and mass of antlers. Top racks are also quite symmetrical from side to side. To make the B&C book, a buck must score at least 195 points. By contrast, the average mature trophy described earlier will score 145 or 150.

Deliberately bagging a buck scoring 185 B&C points or above requires a pocketful of four-leaf clovers plus expert antler-judging ability. Such a buck should have massive antlers with bases nearly as thick as a man's wrists. Most B&C mule deer measure 5 to 6 inches in circumference just below the eyeguards. All four typical points on a record-sized mulie must be exceptionally long. A buck with points shorter than his ears will not make B&C.

Record-Book Mule Deer

A record-book mulie must have massive antlers with bases nearly as thick as a man's wrists. Most B&C mulies measure 5 to 6 inches in circumference below the eyeguards. The main beams are 26 to 28 inches in length; inside spread is 24 to 28 inches.

Sportsmen commonly believe that tremendous antler spread is the key to record-sized bucks. Some regional big-buck contests perpetuate this myth by awarding first prize to the widest outside antler spread. However, a great spread is the least important attribute of a record-book mule deer, and might actually knock the animal out of contention.

For example, scoring rules require that the inside spread be no greater than the length of the main beam. If a big deer has 28-inch beams and a 30-inch inside spread, a penalty is deducted. Outward-thrusting ''cheater'' tines can considerably increase outside antler spread, but the total length of these non-typical points is deducted from the final B&C score. Many impressive, potential record-book mule deer have missed making the book because of extra, spread-enhancing tines.

Typical mule-deer bucks in the 180- to 200-B&C class normally have main beams 26 to 28 inches in length and inside spreads of 24 to

28 inches. When viewed from the side, the main beams usually jut even with or beyond the nose. When facing you, such a buck has main beams spreading 3 or 4 inches beyond each eartip. If such a buck is running away, his antlers extend dramatically beyond the sides of his body. The rack also appears nearly as high as it is wide. Low or shallow antlers with acceptable spreads almost always have short main beams and/or primary points. This severely reduces the score.

If you wish to bag a record-sized mule deer buck with archery tackle, finding such a specimen will be much easier. The P&Y minimum for typical mule deer is 145, which means that any mature, representative 4x4 with or without eyeguards is apt to qualify.

One other note on mule-deer quality: To some experienced hunters, "standard" trophies are not necessarily best. For example, a mule deer with a 30-inch outside spread is the magical goal of many woodsmen—no matter how the rack scores. Mule deer with racks wider than 40 inches are bagged from time to time, and these tend to be impressive prizes regardless of the official score. Similarly, some mature mule deer never grow more than three primary points per side, and few of these attain the awesome length and/or spread.

If you spot a 30-inch wide, massive-beamed 3x3 standing beside a 24-inch, slender-tined 4x4, which would you shoot? The 4x4 would certainly not be my choice.

Coues' Deer

The Coues' deer is North America's smallest officially recognized antlered trophy. On average, a mature buck weighs less than 100 pounds and sports a tight, short-tined basket rack that appears almost "cute" compared to antlers on northern white-tailed deer.

This desert-dwelling animal is in fact a white-tailed deer, but displays physiological characteristics distinctly different from other white-tailed strains. For this reason, the Coues' deer is classified as a separate trophy by all major record-keeping organizations.

The Coues' deer inhabits a relatively small range, thriving in arid and semi-arid environments throughout central and southern Arizona, southwestern New Mexico and northern Mexico.

This animal's small size and geographical isolation serves to limit its popularity with nonresident hunters. However, most serious sportsmen who try Coues' deer are instantly and solidly hooked on the experience.

Often referred to as "the gray ghost of the desert," the Coues' deer enjoys a well-deserved reputation for hunting difficulty—partly because it is unusually alert and skittish, partly because its mouse-gray hide blends perfectly with desert colorations.

Coues' deer are most often spotted from a distance through powerful optics, then stalked and shot in their beds or on the run. Unlike "regular" whitetails, they sometimes bed in semi-open terrain and shun bottomland thickets altogether. Coues' bucks may be small in physical size, but they more than compensate by providing a supreme hunting challenge. Many hunters regard the Coues' deer as our continent's most elusive trophy species.

In some areas, Coues' deer and desert mule deer inhabit the same range. However, these species are distinctly different in appearance.

Coues' deer are light gray in color, with a uniformly gray head and brow reminiscent of other white-tailed subspecies. The muzzle and eyes are lightly ringed with white, and a faint off-white patch is often visible beneath the chin. A Coues' deer's gray-brown tail seems unnaturally long and fluffy, often hanging to the hocks. When this deer runs, it raises its flag in classic white-tailed fashion, revealing a stark-white underside.

By comparison, a desert mule deer is darker gray in color, has a brown-black forehead and usually displays distinct, double patches of white on the throat and lower neck. In addition, a desert mule deer has a prominent white rump patch and a short, white, rope-like tail tipped with black.

Other physical traits aside, a Coues' buck's antlers set it sharply apart from desert mulies and other official types of deer.

Unlike mule deer, a Coues' buck sports a miniature, whitetail-like basket rack with all tines rising from forward-thrusting, sharply curving main beams. A representative, non-record trophy carries three primary tines per side plus eyeguards. This "eight-point" rack will appear tiny to white-tailed deer hunters from the East and Midwest. A Coues' deer measures about 17 inches between the eartips, and an average trophy rack will be narrower than the ears. Outside antler spreads of 12 to 14 inches are respectable. When viewed from the side, a trophy Coues' rack extends forward to the bridge of the nose. Main beams are 13 to 16 inches long. The back tines average 5 to 7 inches in length, and the middle tines measure 2 to 4 inches in length. Eyeguards vary considerably in length, but tend to be relatively short compared to those on regular white-tailed racks. Average eyeguards are 2 to 3 inches long.

Coues' bucks rarely grow 10-point typical racks. Most often, they remain eight-pointers throughout their lives. Representative eight-point antlers like those just described seldom appear exces-

The desert-dwelling Coues' deer is the smallest of all North American recognized antlered trophies. Although it is a white-tailed deer, it is classified separately because of its different physiological characteristics.

sively massive for their size, but heavy-duty versions are sometimes encountered.

Antler coloration varies considerably, but medium gray is the norm. Dark-brown antlers can appear more massive than they actually are.

A good, mature Coues' buck scores between 85 and 100 points on the B&C scale. Such a deer makes a fine archery trophy, easily beating the P&Y minimum of 60. Most Coues' deer riflemen regard a 95-point deer as excellent—a fine head for the wall. However, such an animal falls noticeably short of the current B&C minimum of 110 points.

A genuine Coues' super-trophy is an animal apart. Time worn advice for trophy hunters is "you'll know 'em when you see 'em," and that most assuredly is the case when it comes to record-book Coues'. Such a buck most often sports three primary tines per side plus eyeguards. Beyond this, the similarity with average bucks disappears.

Antlers extend nearly as wide as the eartips, and beams are noticeably longer than the norm. When viewed from the side, a B&C rack extends forward to the tip of the nose, and primary tines rise high above the main beam. Back tines are commonly 8 to 10 inches long, and middle tines often exceed 6 inches. Eyeguards vary considerably in length, but average 4 to 6 inches in height. Though relatively rare, genuine 5x5 (10-point) Coues' bucks score the best for B&C. An extra tine on each side can boost a trophy score by 10 or 12 points—enough to differentiate a nice 100-point deer from a record-class, 110-point buck.

Coues' bucks of B&C size sometimes make the grade on extreme antler mass alone. An average, mature buck has antler bases 3½ inches in circumference. By contrast, many B&C bucks carry antlers with bases to tips of their beams, and can easily score four to six points above normal.

In decent Coues' buck country, you'll see only two or three branch-antlered deer per day—which means that quick trophy-assessing skills is a hard-earned ability. However, you can short-cut this process by paying strict attention to antler width compared to the ears, and main-beam length compared to head length when viewed from the side. Any animal with ear-wide antlers, back tines 8 inches long, middle tines 6 inches long and main beams thrusting forward to the nose is a buck to be proud of. If the deer displays even longer tines, an extra typical tine per side, eyeguards over 3 inches long, and/or unusually massive antlers, it could be a B&C contender!

Record-Book Coues' Deer

The best record-book Coues' deer would be a 10-pointer. Its back tines are 8 to 10 inches long; middle tines are 6 inches. Eyeguards average 4 to 6 inches in height. When viewed from the side, a record-book Coues' rack extends forward to the tip of the nose.

Giant Coues' bucks have been harvested from all parts of this deer's range; however, it seems that Arizona dominates in the trophy-production department.

The Coues' deer is not a large animal, but trophy value is subjective. If high challenge and hard hunting appeal to you, this little customer is impossible to beat!

Columbia Blacktails

Columbia black-tailed deer inhabit a long, narrow range extending from central California northward to the southern tip of Alaska. These are strictly West Coast animals, living within 200 miles of the Pacific Ocean. In addition to booming populations in California, Oregon, Washington and southern British Columbia, a small transplanted herd is doing well in Hawaii. The Columbia blacktail's primary range is bordered on the south and east by mule deer, and on the north by Sitka blacktails.

Columbia blacktails are actively pursued by local sportsmen. These deer are also favored by an avid contingent of nonresident trophy hunters.

Columbia blacktails and mule deer belong to the same species, but a blacktail is significantly smaller in antler and body size. On average, a mature buck is a fine-boned animal weighing 130 to 140 pounds on the hoof. This deer's popularity stems in large part from its wily, elusive nature. The blacktail has much in common with the white-tailed deer, adapting readily to heavy cover and hiding effectively near human habitation. A big blacktail is one of North America's most difficult trophies.

One engaging trait of Columbia blacktails is their preference for widely diverse terrain. No matter what your favorite hunting style, there's a hotspot for you.

Several herds in California and Oregon spend summers above timberline, and migrate to lower winter range in early fall. Many populations live year-round in coastal rain forests, logging clear-cuts or brush-covered foothills. In northern California, these deer abound in warm, semi-open areas with grass and scattered trees. Most foliage-choked river valleys hold huntable herds near alfalfa fields, grainfields and fruit orchards. Such variety lets you stalk, jump-shoot, still-hunt, drive-hunt or stand-hunt to your heart's content.

Columbia blacktails carry antlers shaped like those of mule deer. Most trophy bucks sport bifurcated antlers with four primary tines per side. Eyeguards are present on some racks, but one or both are often missing. Most coastal hunters call a 4x4 blacktail a "four-pointer," counting the four primary tines on one side and ignoring the eyeguards.

A decent, mature Columbia blacktail carries antlers nearly as wide as its 17-inch eartip span. When viewed from the front, this deer's rack appears almost as high as it is wide. Individual antler points seldom measure more than 5 inches. Beams are often spindly compared to their length. A nice, non-record Columbia blacktail seldom gives the impression of extreme antler mass compared to length of tines.

A few stand-out trophies carry only three primary points per side. The middle tine on such deer is often more than 6 inches long. Viewed from the side, the main beams would extend to the bridge of the nose.

A buck of that caliber has main beams 16 to 19 inches in length, eyeguards one or 2 inches long and antler bases 3 to 4 inches in circumference. Such a deer will score 95 to 125 B&C points. This buck

The Columbia blacktail belongs to the same species as the mule deer. However, the Columbia blacktail is smaller in antler and body size. A West Coast animal, the Columbia blacktail prefers widely diverse terrain. It can be a difficult trophy to acquire.

will also exceed P&Y's 90-point minimum.

Non-typical black-tailed bucks are uncommon—so rare, in fact, that record books do not include a non-typical scoring category. However, nice bucks fail to make B&C or P&Y books because they lack sufficient symmetry. Deer with 3x4 or 4x5 antlers are often encountered. These can be impressive, but seldom make the books.

The present B&C minimum score for Columbia blacktails is 130. A buck approaching this size resembles an average mule deer in antler dimension and shape. When first seen, such a buck's antlers seem out of place atop his small, fine-boned head. The rack is apt to be wider than the eartips, and rises unusually high above the head. When viewed from the side, main beams extend forward to the back of the nose. Antlers are often quite massive compared to their length. Eyeguards may or may not be present. There are almost always four primary points per side, and all will measure 3 to 8 inches in length. A giant 3x3 buck occasionally makes B&C, but the deer must possess very long middle tines on each side. Most B&C blacktails are extremely symmetrical, with left and right antlers identical.

The average B&C Columbia blacktail has 20-inch main beams, antler bases 4½ to 5 inches in circumference and four primary tines per side measuring 5 inches in length. Eyeguards are 2 to 4 inches long. The inside spread on such a buck is 17 inches, with outside spread up to 22 inches.

The very best B&C blacktails are absolutely tremendous. Several of these deer score over 170 B&C points.

To harvest a trophy-sized Columbia black-tailed buck, concentrate in proven large-rack areas. Many Pacific Coast locations have deer but no big bucks. Some areas lack genetics or feed for the bucks to grow oversized antlers. More commonly, hunting pressure prevents bucks from reaching trophy age. Today, many record-sized blacktails are bagged in remote wilderness areas or taken on large private ranches with controlled harvest quotas. Oversized bucks are also shot in ultra-dense rain forest zones interspersed with lush logging clearcuts.

California dominates the B&C book, with Oregon and Washington following not far behind. British Columbia also has had many record-book racks.

Despite these statistics, Oregon is presently the best bet for trophy-class blacktails. Since 1980, this state has produced slightly more record heads than California. Washington has declined dramatically in trophy production since 1980, with barely 10 percent of the total yield.

Record-Book Columbia Blacktail

A record-book Columbia blacktail resembles an average mule deer. Most record blacktails have extremely symmetrical antlers. The main beams are 20 inches long; antler base is 4½ to 5 inches in circumference. The four primary tines per side are 5 inches long; eyeguards are 2 to 4 inches.

The two best bets for a giant blacktail are private-lease hunting in northwestern California and rut-hunting along clearcuts in southern and central Oregon. In addition, a few huge California deer are bagged each year in roadless wilderness areas of Mendocino, Trinity and Siskiyou counties. Spot-and-stalk hunting and jump-shooting predominate in California. In Oregon, the up-and-coming tactic is rattling bucks near areas with concentrations of fresh antler rubs. It is extremely important for hunters to learn new techniques that have proven successful.

Hunting black-tailed deer is a first-rate pastime. These animals are not large by mule-deer standards, but they possess a whitetail's cunning and preference for cover. If you desire a genuine trophy buck, be prepared for an enormous hunting challenge.

Sitka Blacktails

Until recently, Sitka black-tailed deer were largely overlooked

The Sitka black-tailed deer is found in Alaska and British Columbia. Although its antler size is small, its body is quite large. This makes field-judging trophy Sitka blacktails quite difficult.

by hunters from "the lower 48." Things changed dramatically in the early 1980s when Boone and Crockett and Pope and Young both recognized these animals as a separate category. The Sitka's remote, far-northern orientation continues to limit hunter participation, but hundreds of sportsmen now trek to deer habitat in coastal Alaska and British Columbia.

Sitka seasons and bag limits are uncommonly liberal. Alaska allows deer hunting without a guide from the first of August through early January, with a yearly bag limit of four or five. B.C.'s Queen Charlotte Islands are the only official Sitka habitat outside Alaska, and black-tailed deer swarm both Graham Island and Moresby Island. The B.C. Sitka season runs from June through mid-winter of the following year, with an annual bag limit of 10 deer. Nonresident deer hunters must have a guide in B.C.

The antlers on the best Sitka bucks often double-branch (bifurcate) in typical mule-deer fashion. Local hunters call such trophies five-pointers, counting the four primary points plus the eyeguard. Most mature Sitka bucks never sprout a fourth point from the back tine, which results in a 4x4 rack similar in shape to that of a small eight-point whitetail. Eyeguards seldom are more than 3 inches long—a trait typical of Columbia blacktails and mule deer.

Uninitiated sportsmen believe that Sitka bucks are undersized in body and antlers. These deer do carry small racks, but their bodies are deceptively large. Mature bucks often exceed 160 pounds on the hoof, while some official weights exceed 200 pounds. The contrast of large bodies and small antlers makes judging difficult.

Alaska and coastal B.C. allow either-sex blacktail hunting, but most nonresidents travel north with trophy bucks in mind. You can legally carry two or three deer tags afield.

An average buck, 3½ to 4½ years old, carries three main points per side plus eyeguards. Such a rack has an outside spread of 12 to 15 inches, back tines 5 to 8 inches long, middle tines 2 to 4 inches long and eyeguards ½ to 2 inches long. When viewed from the side, main beams thrust forward within 2 or 3 inches of the nose. Beams are typically 12 to 14 inches long.

The average Sitka buck measures 17 inches from eartip to eartip when ears are flared alertly ahead. Consequently, most nice, non-record trophy racks appear significantly narrower than the ears. Antler mass on such deer is good, but not excessive, with bases measuring about 3 inches in circumference. Chest depth, body width and other traditional indicators are worthless on Sitka because body size dwarfs the largest rack.

On occasion, run-of-the-mill Sitka bucks carry double-branched, 5x5 antlers. These make desirable trophies, but seldom score significantly higher than 4x4s of equal dimension. Spike or fork-horn antlers are considered substandard, although large 2x2s with eyeguards will squeak into the P&Y record book. Many Sitka bucks carry uneven racks, with 3x4s and 4x5s quite common. True non-typical racks are almost unheard of. Asymmetrical racks make nice wallhangers, but seldom score well enough for the record books.

Symmetrical, middle-sized Sitka racks score 85 to 100 B&C points. Such deer will exceed the P&Y record-book minimum of 75, but it takes something special to beat B&C's minimum of 108.

In establishing a cutoff score, B&C studied hundreds of entries in local Alaskan big-buck contests. In arriving at the 108-point figure, they set a standard as tough to meet as any other B&C deer minimum.

Most bottom-end B&C Sitkas are symmetrical 5x5s. A few long-tined 4x4 bucks have also scored above 108. Such magnum racks usually spread as wide as a buck's eartips and carry extreme mass from bases to tips of tines. Viewed from the side, main beams thrust forward within an inch or two of the nose. These beams generally measure 15 to 18 inches in length. All eight main points extend 2½ to 5 inches beyond the fork, and eyeguards are 2 to 3 inches long. A skillful hunter can probably see 10 to 30 bucks a day in decent habitat, and when a record-breaker appears, the difference is immediately apparent!

Once they lose their velvet, Sitka antlers take on a dark-brown coloration as bucks rub their racks on doghair-thick coastal undergrowth. A massive, deeply-stained rack with polished ivory tips is beautiful.

Several Sitkas exceeding 120 points have been harvested by riflemen. Some Sitka blacktail areas produce larger bucks than others. Kodiak Island, Alaska, dominates the record books. However, Prince of Wales Island and the Alaskan mainland near Ketchikan have also produced some top-flight trophies. Other locales like Admiralty Island and B.C.'s Queen Charlotte Islands harbor oodles of deer, but come up short in the record-book department.

Hunting pressure is not a factor in determining Sitka trophy size because most areas are underharvested. According to northern biologists, winter and spring conditions largely determine average yearly antler growth. Serious trophy deer hunters should monitor late-winter and early-spring weather patterns before planning their Sitka adventures.

Thanks to long deer seasons in Alaska and British Columbia, a

Record-Book Sitka Blacktail

Most record-book Sitka blacktails carry extremely massive racks, spreading as wide as a buck's eartips. From the side, main beams reach within an inch or so of the nose; the beams are about 15 to 18 inches long. The eight main points are 2½ to 5 inches beyond the fork; eyeguards are 2 to 3 inches.

variety of hunting techniques can be used between midsummer and late fall.

Sportsmen who prefer to backpack can spot-and-stalk bachelor groups of high-country bucks throughout August and early September. Sitka bucks shed their antler velvet in late August, so earlier hunts do not produce fully formed trophy racks.

Another favorite hunting time for giant bucks is late October through mid-November. The rut is in full swing, and mature bucks are cruising the countryside all day, searching for receptive does.

During heavy snow years, Sitka bucks sometimes congregate along ocean beaches in late November and early December. This can allow easy stalking or hunting from boats.

Local gunners harvest Sitka deer into January, but trophy hunters should beware. Sitka bucks drop antlers in December, making winter trips a waste of time.

In addition to stalking and still-hunting, giant Sitka bucks are suckers for bleating-fawn calls. Deer-calling in densely wooded areas has been the undoing of many wall-hanger bucks in southern Alaska and northern B.C. However, fawn-bleating is foolhardy on Kodiak Island and other places where Alaskan brown bear abound.

Sitka deer are first-rate big-game animals. What they lack in antler size they more than make up for in beauty, solid hunting enjoyment and great meat on the table.

Non-Typical Bucks

Giant typical bucks are magnificent, but record-sized non-typical bucks are astonishing. Such an animal sports a huge typical rack adorned with extra tines sprouting in every direction. This "gingerbread" is guaranteed to turn the head of any serious hunter.

Non-typical deer are far less common than typical bucks. Populations of whitetails, Coues' deer and mule deer produce enough giant, abnormal racks to warrant separate record-book categories. Blacktails, on the other hand, rarely grow true non-typical antlers. A few blacktails have short tines in unusual places, but almost never display enough extra bone to appear radically unusual. For this reason, major world-record organizations, like the Boone and Crockett Club and Pope and Young Club, do not recognize non-typical Sitka and Columbia black-tailed deer.

The way record-scoring systems are set up, there are really four kinds of big deer racks. Typical antlers are large and incredibly symmetrical from side to side. Non-typical antlers must also be symmetrical to make the record lists. These possess the basic side-to-side symmetry of a typical record head plus plenty of extra bone in the form of outward-thrusting "cheater" drop tines from the main beam, extra eyeguards and other tines appearing in unusual places.

The third and fourth types of deer racks don't make anybody's record list, but can be quite impressive in their own right. One variety is big and typical in antler structure, but has just enough extra tine development to throw it out of typical record-book categories. Mule deer are especially prone to grow such antlers—big, even racks with two to six short, extra points per side.

The other variety has little or no symmetry from side to side. One main beam might be short and the other long, or one side might have twice as many tines as the other. Physical injury sometimes will cause deer to grow such racks.

The two types of antlers just described are seen in both mule and white-tailed deer populations, and most hunters will deck such animals in a heartbeat. However, in order to make the record books, you

Non-typical bucks are magnificent. Their racks astonish serious hunters and make majestic trophies. The non-typical deer has a typical rack with extra tines growing in almost every direction.

must look for a particular type of non-typical buck.

Let's take whitetails as an example. A non-typical B&C contender must have two characteristics. First, the basic rack must be huge and typical, with long main beams, high-rising eyeguards and four or more normal tines per side. The inside spread of the main beams should be 19 to 24 inches wide.

Second, a record-sized, non-typical whitetail must carry substantial extra bone in the form of non-typical tines. On average, the rack must have at least 25 or 30 inches of extra tine length. Fifteen extra tines, all 2 inches long, might be enough for the deer to make the list. Two 8-inch drop tines plus two extra 7-inch eyeguards might also do the trick. Non-typical antler development varies considerably from rack to rack.

The B&C non-typical white-tailed deer minimum score is 195— that's 25 points above the typical minimum. As a result, any buck with a 170-point typical rack plus 30 inches of non-typical tines will make B&C with a score of 200. By comparison, a 170-point typical rack with only 10 or 15 inches of non-typical tines won't make any record list because the extra tines must be deducted from the typical score. Sad to say, these extra tines do not add up sufficiently to make the non-typical minimum, either.

The same basic judging guidelines apply to Coues' deer and mule deer. If you see a non-typical buck, the first step is ascertaining the deer's typical antler structure. If the animal appears to be record-book size without its extra tines, you should then add up the estimated length of all non-typical tines. Mule deer must carry 45 or 50 inches of extra tine length to meet the 240-point B&C non-typical minimum. Coues' deer usually require only 10 or 15 inches of extra tine length to make the B&C non-typical minimum of 120.

The P&Y bowhunter's record book also recognizes non-typical bucks from white-tailed, Coues' and mule-deer populations. The minimums are merely scaled down. Non-typical white-tailed bucks must score 150—25 points above the typical minimum of 125. Non-typical mule deer must score 160—15 points above the typical minimum of 145. Coues' bucks must score 66—6 points above the typical minimum of 60.

If an abnormal buck has a typical antler frame of record-book size plus enough inches of extra tines, the animal just might make the non-typical list.

Non-typical bucks are extremely difficult to judge. Abnormal tines often curve or jut in strange directions, making length estimation a difficult chore. Dark antlers seem especially massive, and

Record-Book Non-Typical Whitetail

The record books recognize non-typical bucks in the white-tailed, mule and Coues' categories; however, because blacktails are rarely non-typical, the record book does not recognize the Columbia or Sitka black-tailed species. Non-typical bucks are extremely difficult to judge.

light-colored racks tend to make tines look longer than they really are. Only a long, calm look through binoculars or a spotting scope will give you a chance of reasonably close assessment.

Fortunately, a non-typical record-book contender always looks huge on the hoof. Nobody I know would hesitate to shoot such a deer at first glance. The only exceptions is spot-and-stalk mule deer hunting, where long-distance, cross-canyon deer viewing forces a deliberate choice.

Some hunters believe non-typical records are caused by injury to the animal. This is almost never the case because such deer must be very typical in basic antler structure. Body or head injuries usually affect only one side of a rack, creating grotesque non-symmetry and making a high score impossible. A huge, palmated, multi-pointed antler on one side with a feeble, curved spike or withered fork on the other certainly denotes a ''non-typical'' buck. However, the rack's lack of symmetry will prevent it from making the record books.

Experts agree that genetics are largely responsible for giant, non-typical deer racks. Hunters sometimes find shed antlers from the same white-tailed or mule deer year after year, and these usually appear quite similar throughout the animal's mature life. Pen-raised non-typical bucks also display consistent genetic programming through consistent, repetitive antler growth.

Some areas will yield more non-typical deer antlers than others. For example, Montana is the foremost producer of typical and non-typical B&C whitetails in the Rocky Mountain West. However, typical deer tend to appear in eastern and north-central parts of the state. The extreme northwest corner yields a disproportionate number of abnormal, record-sized racks. This phenomenon can only be explained by genetics. Similarly, some mule-deer states are clearly better for non-typical deer than others.

Wyoming, New Mexico and Colorado have all produced B&C non-typicals, but the majority of record bucks have been typical. In contrast, Arizona, Alberta, California and Montana have produced significantly more non-typicals than typicals of record size. To deliberately bag a non-typical wall-hanger, you must study the record books and concentrate your efforts where such animals are most likely to appear.

The B&C book lists more typical racks in every deer category than non-typical specimens. In the P&Y book there are eight times as many typical mule deer listed as non-typical heads, and 14 times as many typical whitetails listed as non-typical deer. Any giant buck is something to be excited about and proud of, but big non-typicals are the rarest of the rare!

5

Improving Hunting Accuracy
by Hal Swiggett

What is hunting accuracy? We must define it before we can improve it. Ask a dozen hunters and you'll get at least a dozen answers. To the majority, hunting accuracy usually means three shots in 4 or 5 inches. More often than not at 100 yards, but sometimes at only half that distance. Many times it's, "I haven't shot this gun since last season. All I need to find out is if it's still on the paper." They take one or two shots, and if either hits the paper they usually come out with, "Yep, she's right where she was last year," and away they go.

I'm not out to ruffle feathers, but the average hunter simply does not shoot enough to know how well his rifle, handgun or muzzleloader performs. All of the handgun hunters I know personally shoot hundreds of rounds before going on a hunt. The muzzleloading fraternity I used to be around shot constantly. Not hundreds of times like smokeless powder folks do, but enough to know what their rifle will do and, beyond that, what they can do with that rifle. There is a difference.

Years ago, I wrote that I had cleaned my last black-powder gun. I meant it, too. Thompson/Center folks are known to be sneaky. They came up with their in-line Scout rifle and pistol. I was coerced into trying the short one, and killed a rather nice eight-point whitetail with it.

Why did I go back?

This Scout pistol was the first ever that could digest a full rifle charge of the smelly stuff.

Now you know how to improve your hunting accuracy. First you shoot, then you shoot some more and when you've finished go back and start over. That's what I do and this bald-headed old typewriter jockey has been shooting for over 65 years.

Safari Hunting

When I go on safari in South Africa, I take my 7½-inch .454 Casull and a 14-inch .375 JDJ (custom SSK Industries barrel on a T/C frame). They are always ready. The .454 prints 2 inches high at 50 yards and still 1½ inches high at 100 yards. Unless forced, its hammer will not be dropped on anything beyond 150 yards. If I hold where I want to hit, I'm home free. The .375 is 4½ inches high at 100 yards and dead on at 200. It is 18 inches low at 300. I know this from actually shooting more than a few times at these distances. Again, unless forced, that T/C hammer will not be dropped beyond that particular point.

Even with all this behind me, those two guns will still be fired 15 or 20 times a week until I board that South Africa Airways airplane at John F. Kennedy airport in New York. Yes, I take shooting at animals seriously.

Cap And Ball Revolvers

Cap and ball revolvers, as far as hunting is concerned, are capable of only small-game hunting. Cottontails, squirrels and maybe a called-in-close fox on occasion are fair game. Though I've never taken a fox with one, a lone bobcat did succumb to a .45 ball (.44 revolvers use .45 balls; .45 rifles use .44 balls) over 30 grains of 3 F black. This is a Remington replica. I thought I was calling gray fox but this cat let curiosity get the best of him. The shot was at 17 steps.

Big-Game Rifles

Hunting rifles intended for big game were .50, .54 and .58 so far as I was concerned. Many big-game animals are taken with .45s; however, knowing .44 round balls weigh about 128 grains, I've always leaned toward more weight.

In the Tennessee mountains, I was stalking whatever might make itself visible in a downright hard rain—downpour better describes the situation. A Catalina goat suddenly appeared out of nowhere. He wasn't far off and seemed confused. After peeling the cling wrap off the nipple of my .50 caliber Thompson/Center rifle and carefully

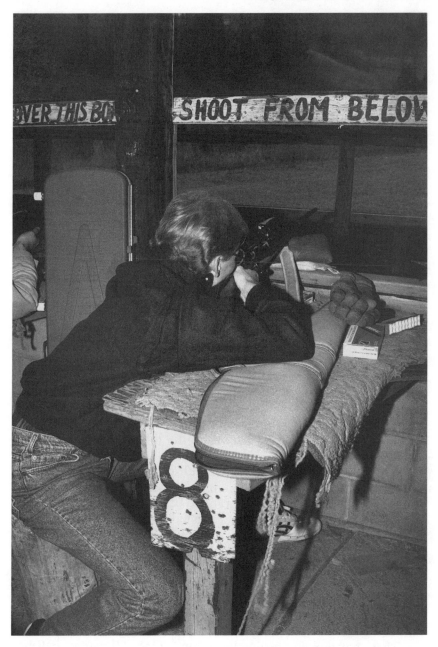

Improving hunting accuracy begins with shooting often; the more practice time and rounds you put in, the better. Hunters should shoot from various positions and at different targets. Bench shooting is just one form of practice.

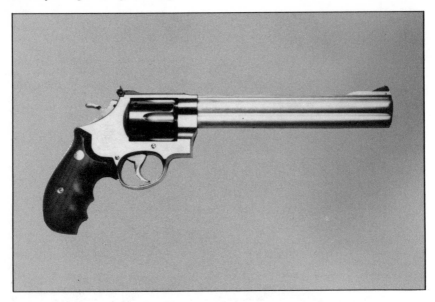

Whether using a modern handgun like this S&W 629 Classic or an old-time cap and ball revolver, field shooting will improve hunting accuracy.

aiming at his shoulder, I pulled the trigger. Once the smoke cleared, no goat was in sight; however, my heart shot was plainly visible on a small tree. That was when I discovered my rifle was a true single shot. I mean one shot and back to the barn. During that continuing downpour, its wooden ramrod had swollen to the point it could not be removed. Pliers and strong hands did the job once we got back to headquarters.

A long time ago, a few hunters felt compelled to try two balls over a charge. This was no problem if the balls were in solid contact. If not, "Hang on, George, it's going to be rough from here on out!" I tried this method once, because I wanted to see the effect of two .50 caliber balls on an animal. I went meat hunting for a white-tailed doe. The shot was fired at approximately 50 yards. She was near broadside. It was a still day—not even a slight breeze. In other words, the smoke held tight. When I could see there was no deer in sight, I went to where she had been standing. Her hindquarters were visible between a couple of small cedars. They were on the ground—stretched out, actually.

That shot proved absolutely nothing. One .50 caliber ball had gone through her heart; the other through her liver. Either one is deadly. I never tried again.

Muzzleloading Rifles

Hunters using black powder must already know that lighter charges usually give better accuracy. Never discount the possible accuracy of muzzleloading rifles. The shooter who is willing to experiment with ball sizes and patch thickness, along with varying powder charges, will discover extreme accuracy.

Some find Pyrodex very fascinating—I did. After working with fireworks and movie and special effects materials with black powder, Dan Pawlak became dissatisfied with the powder's performance and safety and decided to design a better substance to do the same job. Though an explosion at his Pyrodex plant took his life, he did accomplish his goal. I still use Pyrodex and prefer it over black powder.

Because of Pyrodex' different density, it can be used with measure settings at your usual black-powder amounts. Do not increase Pyrodex or black-powder charges. Stick to whatever your source says is maximum. If you go beyond the amounts recommended by your source, all you will be doing is fertilizing the area—the excess exits the muzzle with the ball. Usually, the best accuracy comes from a slightly reduced charge. Match shooters normally use the smallest amount of powder that will get their ball to the target.

I took the first American bison (buffalo) in modern times with a

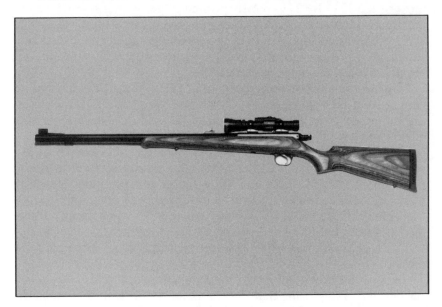

Finding the best load for a muzzleloader like this Knight MK-85 may take a lot of experimentation. However, the end result will be tack-driving accuracy.

muzzleloader on Joe McKnight's ranch in New Mexico. It was done with the Navy Arms "Buffalo Hunter," a .58 caliber. My projectile was the 505-grain mini-ball. The charge was 100 grains of 2 F and that first shot was about 70 yards. The bull was young, about 2½ years old. The New Mexico sun was hot—very hot. Joe's buffalo were not cooperative. Most of the time was spent trying to get a young bull to hold still long enough for the shot. (My mini-ball was stuffed with cooking shortening).

When we finally singled out a 2½-year-old willing to cooperate, I very carefully aimed for the center of his lungs, pulled the trigger and heard a loud "PFFFT." The mini-ball hit the prairie grass halfway to where the bull stood. My shortening had melted to the point that it killed most of the charge. Fortunately, it left enough charge to get my 505-grain hunk of lead out of the barrel. The buffalo? He thought the whole show was rather amusing. He watched as I poured 100 grains of 2 F in and another shortening-filled mini-ball.

Shooting At The Range

Years ago, while visiting a local range, I changed some targets at the 100-yard mark, and slipped in two new ones at 50 yards. One of these targets was unbelievable; there were seven holes scattered over most of the 17½ by 21½ paper (printed target with a 12-inch center and four 6-inch corners). All seven bullets had hit full sideways—flat at 50 yards. I don't have the vaguest idea who did it. Since deer season opened two days later, I assumed that the rifle went hunting. After all, seven shots were on the paper.

One of my close friends received a .270 Wthby Mag. just before deer season. He wanted me to go with him to sight it in. At the shooting range, my friend's rifle proved to be well on the paper, rather close to center. The rifle had been used before. My friend seemed a bit shy of his new deer rifle. This apprehension could have been because he thought the Weatherby's high-velocity reputation meant more recoil. A few shots and adjustments for wind and elevation made me believe it was as close as we could get it for him.

Finally, in sort of desperation, I asked, "Do you have any ammo left? If so, I would like to try a couple of shots."

"There are four left in this box and I have another in my car," he replied.

Snuggling down behind his Weatherby and checking his scope for parallax assured me that there was no problem in that area. His effort was keeping shots within 4 to 5 inches. The center, however, stayed where I wanted him to be sighted in. My first shot printed ½

Navy Arms .58 caliber "Buffalo Hunter" claimed this Sika deer, which holds the world record extra-typical in Burkett Trophy Game Records. A 505-grain mini-ball and 100 grains of 2 F was used.

inch right and 3 inches high. The second was ¾ inch below and left. The third was ¾ inch directly above the last shot. My fourth shot, the last cartridge in the box, printed slightly left and almost between those last two for elevation. The entire group was barely over 1¼ inches. Maybe closer to 1½, but a lot better than I expected from his rifle. Without moving his eye from the spotting scope, he said, "Hal, don't do this to me." Then he added, "I guess I just need to shoot more."

He summed up everything in those words. Most shooters just need to shoot more to improve accuracy.

I'm not an expert bench-shooter and have never claimed to be. Years of experience helped me develop a technique. One reason for my amount of experience is that I seldom have a rifle long enough to really get to know it. My friend Robert Kleinguenther builds custom rifles. He guarantees three shots in ½ inch at 100 yards with approved loads. Each rifle does this or it doesn't leave his shop. I have helped him, many times, shoot those groups. Years ago, Winchester invited several writers to East Alton to introduce its new Supreme ammunition line. The invitation included, "Bring your most accurate rifle and see how our Supreme shoots in it." They specified calibers available. I knew Robert Kleinguenther had finished a .300 Win. Mag. for a customer. I told him about the invitation, and he immediately began working to have one ready for me. Before dark on the evening before my flight to St. Louis, he put the rifle through its paces and declared it ready. Not blued, but ready for shooting. I went to his place about 10:30 that night and got it.

Because I've spent years on public ranges, I've become cautious. I settled on the extreme left-end bench. My first shot on their range was at a small stick on the bank behind the target. The 10X scope helped the bullet hit 2 inches low. Another shot at another stick produced the same result. I took one more shot to be sure, then I moved to the paper. The main concern here was group—not point of impact. The first shot printed 4 inches low and almost that much left; however, it was on the paper, which was the only necessity. Before my second shot, a voice bellowed, "Hold it until I get a spotting scope on your target!" It was a Winchester official. Settling on the bench to my right, he focused in and said, "Go ahead, I'm ready." How would you like to have to shoot under those circumstances?

My second shot went downrange, and he called it out loud, "A little low and left of the first." My third was acknowledged by, "This is beginning to look mighty good." The fourth resulted in, "If he can put this one in the center, he'll have a great group!" I was ready to throw in the towel because he was shouting. What chance was there to see how well my custom rifle could do? Anyway, I had to try.

My fifth shot caused him to leap off that bench shouting for the range to stop shooting so my target could be brought in. His ruler proclaimed it to be .89 inch. The group was photographed. I was photographed with the Winchester official and the group. My name was eventually used in Winchester's advertising.

What does this have to do with improving hunting accuracy? Everything. I could never have done that well if I didn't shoot a lot. The best barrel ever made screwed into a perfect receiver, bedded to perfection and loaded with specifically tuned ammunition won't benefit the shooter who hasn't practiced enough to utilize that perfection. Fifty or 100 shots a year will not turn anyone into a good shot.

Ammunition Accuracy Between Brands

Deer season is approaching and a hunter has shot half a box of ammunition, Winchester 130-grain .270. On the way home, he stops at a sporting goods store for a fresh box. "I need a box of .270s," he says. The clerk normally will ask the brand. More often than not, the reply is "What difference does it make, they're all the same." With this out of the way, the hunter pays for a box of Remington's and is ready for opening day. He has no idea where his rifle will print this ammunition but, after all, it's still .270 and 130-grain so it should be okay. Chances are good that he'll get his deer and never know the point of impact was 3 or 4 inches off from his sighting-in Winchester ammunition.

Shooting Range Vs. Field

Shooting off a bench with sandbags for support and a comfortable stool adjusted to the right height helped sight that rifle in and get that "good" 3- or 4-inch group. Here, I must ask a question. How many deer have you shot from a bench, using sandbags and sitting on a comfortable stool adjusted to the right height?

Few hunters can keep a field group in twice the area that they shoot on a range. Most, by far, will exceed that. If we double the 3- to 4-inch group, it's 6 to 8 inches—still in the chest if the shooter's hold is good. Most hunters in this group will do well, shooting three times (9 to 12 inches) their range group while in the field. This most likely means a gut-shot animal.

Here again, the most accurate rifle in the world won't help if the person holding it can't shoot.

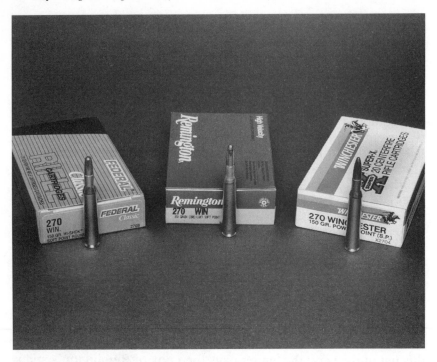

Ammunition from the three top manufacturers, Federal, Remington and Winchester, is shown here. Even though all three boxes contain .270 150-grain ammo, they will not produce the same accuracy if used interchangeably. After sighting in with a specific brand of ammo, continue loading that brand in the field.

Once the rifle is sighted in to the best of your ability, leave that bench and try various positions, such as leaning against a post the way you might use a tree in the woods; sitting with your back against that post for support and putting your elbows on your knees to steady your aim; and, getting down on your knees, using the shooting bench's corner the way you would a stump or rock in the field. Also, fit a hasty sling to your rifle and learn to slip your elbow through it for a shot. A little practice and you'll be surprised how much support this can be. However, don't get involved with military slings; they are for an entirely different purpose.

Rifle Rests

If shooting from a blind or stand, place a jacket, gloves or a hat on the edge, then rest your rifle's forend on that. Never rest any part of your rifle on any solid object. It will shoot away from any solid rest.

In Texas and in many Western states, shots might be taken from a vehicle—usually across the hood. My long-time favorite rifle rest in this situation is my hat. Big western hats have a crease in the top which is ideally suited to hold a rifle's forend (handguns, too, for that matter.)

Never, unless absolutely necessary (meaning a crippled animal), shoot at any animal over 50 or 60 yards without some type of support. Experienced shooters can double that, but they won't pull the trigger unless it's necessary.

Pulling The Trigger

I've used the word *pull* several times; however, hunters have been taught to "squeeze" a trigger. Pick up a salt shaker or some similar-sized object and grip it in your hand as if it were a gun. Squeeze it gently, as if squeezing a trigger. Watch it move. Then, hold the object firmly and gently pull your finger into it. No movement. Another step toward improving hunting accuracy.

Here the hasty sling can be seen in action. Note how the left hand slides tightly against the front swivel. The trick is to have it adjusted so when in this position it is pulled taut.

Handguns, which are lighter and shorter, are more susceptible to movement. Gripping must be firm but not tight. Tense muscles tend to quiver, so triggers must be pulled even more gently. Same reason as above. Big-bore revolvers with heavy bullets tend to both buck and roar. Rifle cartridges in handguns, with their much higher velocity, tend to perform in that same manner.

Handling Recoil

Recoil never hurt anyone, unless it gets out of hand. Use common sense. Hold the gun tight enough so that it won't jump out of your hand, and let it buck and roar.

At the same time, use common sense. For example, a young friend was moving to Alaska. He owned a Thompson/Center Contender and about three barrels. Knowing there were moose in Alaska, I gave him a .45-70 barrel. At the same time, I gave him the load I use in my custom SSK-T/C .45-70 with some basic instructions: Do not try it until 100 rounds of factory ammunition have been fired through the barrel.

A month later, a phone call revealed he had ignored my advice. He had loaded some of the 500-grain bullets (Hornady's .458 Win. Mag. bullets) and proceeded to the range. The first time he fired, the barrel came back and nicked his head. Using his words, ''I knew I could hold that thing down, so I tried again.'' His second shot resulted in a trip to the hospital and seven stitches in his head.

I shoot those bullets regularly and have taken several big-game animals. A few years ago, I shot those loads 107 times in 90 minutes, proving a new pistol scope brought out by Simmons. The first 10 averaged 1,554 feet per second through Oehler's Model 35P chronograph. The remaining 97 were simply shot into the 25-yard backstop. My wrist and elbow hurt for about 10 days, but the scope survived beautifully and is marketed by Simmons today. It is their 2.5-7X.

Handgunning

Rifle cartridges in handguns, primarily bolt-action or falling block (pistols by my definition), will perform the same as they do in longer-barreled rifles. Shots in the 300-yard range are well within reason for the practiced, accomplished and dedicated shooter. Just because a gun has the capability or someone else has done it doesn't mean everyone can pull off those shots. Lots of practice makes those shots possible.

If, with your handgun, you can keep five shots in 4 to 5 inches off a solid bench at 100 yards, you should not be shooting at game be-

Always use binoculars for seeking your target. A rifle scope is attached to a deadly weapon, and it should only be used when you have verified the animal you want to shoot.

yond 50 or 60 yards. Most revolvers won't do any better until tuned by a professional in that field. Handloads can be developed to cut that in half. One of my .44 Magnums is 8⅜ inches of barrel topped with a 2X Bausch & Lomb scope. It will, with 320-grain, hard-cast bullets, consistently put five shots in 2 to 2½ inches over that length of a football field distance—from a solid bench rest. It is a Mag-Na-Port Stalker with work done on a Ruger Super Blackhawk. I believe they provide this same customizing on Model 29 Smith & Wessons, too.

Freedom Arms' .454 Casull will cut that group in half when I do my part. It handles 300-grain, hard-cast bullets. When I go on safari, I switch its 2X Bausch & Lomb scope to a 4X Simmons. The .375 JDJ wears a 2.5-7X Simmons.

Magnification

Many hunters are obsessed with magnification. A 7X on any hunting rifle should be the maximum; 5 or 6X would probably be better.

The 7X brings a 350-yard animal in to 50 yards. More logically, it brings a 100-yard animal into 14¼ yards. This, obviously, is totally impractical. Woods hunters at most should use a 1.5-4X or 5X or, better yet, a 2X.

There is absolutely no place in hunting territory for 3-9X or 4-12X scopes. They are heavier, which means cumbersome to lug up mountains and through brushes. You will seldom find an experienced hunter with such a glass on his rifle.

Scopes are not for spotting animals or checking out movements on yonder hill. You could be aiming a deadly weapon at another hunter. Binoculars—not scopes—are for seeking out targets.

Most new rifles or handguns will shoot better than most hunters; however, many will need a trigger job. I say that because trial lawyers have made it impossible for firearms companies to market their products with good, sensible triggers. Some companies manufacture triggers that cannot be adjusted. You will never shoot a 6- to 8-pound trigger as well as one that lets off 3½ pounds. This 3½ pounds is probably optimum for most hunting rifles. You should never go lighter because you want a light trigger. When you reach that point, you should have a better reason for such an adjustment. I like double-set triggers and have them on several rifles. Big-game rifles are set for 3 to 3½ pounds.

Mechanical Tuning

If your group walks across the target as it is fired, have the bedding checked. If it shoots to a different point of impact from a cold barrel than it did from a slightly heated one (from shooting), the bedding is probably at fault; however, occasionally, a burr might be in the crown causing the problems. As far as overall tuning of new rifles, it is seldom needed. Modern manufacturing of firearms and ammunition has become extremely close to perfection. Thus, blame yourself first for bad groups and misses, then start checking your equipment. You really will be surprised at how much better your rifle or handgun shoots after a few hundred rounds have been put through it.

Factory Vs. Handloading

Ammunition for cartridges developed in the last 50 years is good. Most of the time, handloaders are trying to equal factory results. You would have to do a lot of shooting to improve on what can be bought over the counter.

Accuracy can, in many instances, be improved with handloading; however, you will need to be an accomplished shot. Handload-

Handloading does have its advantages. For one, it helps cut costs. However, only experienced shooters should take this challenge on, and they should always read more than one instructional handloading manual.

ing also helps cut expenses. Buy good equipment and more than one manual. Several manuals are on the market and all are good. Each gives the same advice, but in different ways. You should then start experimenting by changing powders and load density. Often a grain, or even half a grain of powder will make a tremendous difference in group size. You won't be able to notice this until you have learned to keep those holes as close together as possible with what you are already shooting.

Shooting is no different than success in any other field. It takes long hours and hard work. There are no shortcuts. Once you've learned to hold that firearm correctly and pull the trigger gently so that no movement in sight alignment is visible, you have the fundamentals down.

Improving your hunting accuracy means taking advantage of what you already have and learning its capabilities to the fullest. With a lot of hard work (shooting), those rifles in your rack may surprise you. In fact, you may already own a jewel.

6

So You Want A Bull Elk?
by Duane Wiltse

Phenomenal growth in elk herds has occurred in the Rocky Mountain West; more and better bulls are available. Merwin Martin, a cement contractor in Powell, Wyoming, harvested a large bull in Wyoming. The massive seven-point bull was 11½ years old. At the time, this was the second largest bull taken in the state, and it placed eighth in the Boone and Crockett Club record book.

There has never been a better time to plan a Western elk hunt. Your chances for success increase with the increased quantity and quality of elk herds. A successful elk hunt, whether you harvest a bull or not, begins at home at least a year before the trip West.

First, book with a legitimate, licensed and experienced outfitter. Do this as early in the year as possible. Most Western states usually allocate their non-resident elk licenses through some type of drawing early in the year. For example, Wyoming's license application deadline is Feb. 1 of each year.

Another reason for booking early is to get acquainted with the outfitter. The outfitter will want you to know what to expect in his camp and country. Communication is only half the equation. Comprehension is the key for both of you.

Finding an outfitter can be done in the comfort of your own home with a pen and paper or telephone. It can also be done through a booking agency that you have worked with and trust. Booking agents offer some advantages; however, they also tend to isolate the hunter and outfitter from each other. Conventions and sport shows offer excellent opportunities to meet several outfitters so you can make a comparison.

There are hundreds of outfitter advertisements in nearly every hunting and fishing magazine. The NAHC, however, publishes an "approved guides and outfitters" booklet each year. The NAHC updates this booklet regularly; it is an excellent source for finding good, reputable outfitters.

Outfitted elk hunts usually cost from $2,500 to $4,500, depending upon the state and type of hunt, such as wilderness horseback high-country hunts or four-wheel drive ranch hunts. Be sure you know exactly what the fee covers. Does the fee include license or landowner coupons? Are there any additional trophy fees? There will be additional costs, such as transportation from home to wherever you meet your outfitter, food and lodging the night before and the night after your hunt, taxidermy and meat processing. Be sure you fully understand what is included in the base fee. Then, there are no unpleasant surprises for anyone.

You should expect from your outfitter honest answers to your questions, experienced and competent guides, three well-balanced meals per day, a warm and dry place to eat and sleep, dependable equipment such as a four-wheel drive vehicle and experienced, gentle horses with saddles, scabbard and saddlebags in good condition.

You should determine the availability of game from independent sources. An area's harvest records from previous years can be checked by contacting natural resources, forest service or land management personnel.

The most you should expect from an outfitter is to get you into and out of the hunting country in a safe and reasonably comfortable manner. Don't leave your hunting and shooting skills at home. The outfitter and guide are there to assist, coach, direct and encourage you. Even though the habitat, game, elevation and humidity are all new to you, the bulk of your hunting success rests on your shoulders. There is, after all, no instant replay during an elk hunt, and nobody to cover for your lack of research or preparation. It's just you and the fickle elements, the suspicious bull and your guide. If you're lucky, you'll have a small window of opportunity to place a killing shot. Don't be like some of today's hunters who try to substitute technology for discipline, skill and ability.

Frame Of Mind And Commitment

To be a successful elk hunter, you should first be in the proper

A Western elk hunt is one of the most exciting adventures a hunter can experience. However, elk hunts demand extra stamina and skill; therefore, give yourself adequate time to plan and prepare for the hunt.

The price for booking an elk hunt will vary, depending upon the type of hunt. When booking a wilderness horseback high-country hunt with an outfitter, you should expect experienced, gentle horses with quality saddles, scabbard and saddlebags.

frame of mind. If something has happened in your business or family life that causes you to feel uncomfortable about spending the money and time away on this hunt, then by all means postpone the hunt until next year. A good, professional outfitter will give 100 percent of his time and resources toward the hunt. If you can't do the same, then reschedule.

Choose the outfitter who has a good area to hunt and a reputation of being honest, hardworking and professional—someone who always does his best and is successful most of the time. Do not choose one based solely on his success ratio with other clients. Generally speaking, non-resident hunters who book with outfitters enjoy 20 to 25 percent more success than resident hunters without outfitters.

Now it's time to make a commitment to him and yourself. During the 20 years I've been outfitting for trophy bull elk, every hunter I've booked has wanted a six-point bull. The first time we talk on the telephone or in person, he wants me to clearly understand he wants a six-point bull. He says he is prepared to do whatever is necessary: He will buy a new rifle, quit smoking, lose weight, work out, practice on the shooting range ... whatever it takes! During subsequent phone conversations throughout the year, he reminds me that he is the one who wants the six-point bull and plans to get in shape soon. When I meet him the night before his hunt begins, he reminds me again of his need for a six-point bull while apologizing for not losing weight, working out or quitting smoking. He did, however, go out last week and spend a lot of money on a new magnum rifle. Also, he asks if he can shoot it a couple times in the morning while packing the horses because he didn't have time to get to the range.

It's always interesting to witness the process of changing priorities. With some hunters, it directly relates to personal comfort. It usually begins with a tentative "WHOA, WHOA." The hands have been vigorously packing mules and saddling horses for three hours. The mules, horses and hands are anxious to begin the four-hour horseback trip to camp. Suddenly, this hunter finds himself 15 hands from the ground and wants everything to be in slow motion. Two minutes after mounting up we make our first (of many) icy river crossing. He loses his new hat and the water that splashes on him turns into ice droplets within seconds. He clamps a death grip on the saddlehorn as his horse is jostled climbing up the slippery bank. Already his priorities begin to shift. Now, his No. 1 priority is his personal safety—and it should be. That's why you want an outfitter with a good, dependable vehicle, horse and tack. Four hours later as the horses strain for the campsite, the soft, overweight, coughing, cold and stiff (maybe wet if it's been raining or snowing) hunter has changed his second priority to his personal comfort. What do you think he'd have to say if we hadn't had the time to set up the tents yet? Or, if the camptender had been too tired to cut firewood and haul water. Or, if the cook had slept instead of spending the entire day building fires, baking bread and pies and preparing a supper fit for a king?

As our hunter laboriously crawls into his sleeping bag after his first full day of elk hunting, reality begins to seep into his foggy mind. It's 11 p.m. and that devilish guide is going to get him up at 4 a.m. tomorrow so they can ride farther before daylight. This hunter did not understand the hardships of riding in the dark for an hour in the morning and two hours in the evening. He did not know the wind blows all the time in elk country or that those crazy elk hang out in the most unforgiving and slippery terrain imaginable. He does know that he needs to move faster and be more alert and responsive to his guide's instructions if he's going to even see an elk—any elk—on this trip. He can't believe he had an entire year to prepare for this trip and blew it! As an exhaustive sleep begins to flood over him, he decides that any bull at all will be fine. He just hopes he can hit him with that new rifle.

Gear And Confidence

Another aspect of preparation is gear. You will make a very positive impression on the outfitter and guides if you arrive at the trailhead ready to ride with a minimum amount of duffle. You are only going to be there a week to 10 days, so you really don't need that much. Take about six pairs of cotton socks, three pairs of wool socks, a full change of clothes (including long johns), a pair of well-broken-in leather hiking boots, a pair of winter pac boots with extra liners, a wool cap with ear flaps, three pairs of gloves, a wool jacket, a down vest and a good rain slicker. What else do you really need? Okay, maybe a sweater or sweatshirt and neckerchief, camera, binoculars and a good warm sleeping bag. The entire shooting match should fit nicely into one duffle bag (not counting sleeping bag) and weigh no more than 45 pounds. You'll be amazed at how comfortable you can be for a few days with just the basics. Don't be unduly concerned about getting cold, wet, tired or sore. Plan on it! Successful elk hunting is strenuous and hard work at elevations of 7,500 feet or more. Extra gear and gadgets won't help—leave them home.

Arrive with your sense of humor intact and a healthy, positive, confident attitude. You will have that confidence if you are comfortable with your rifle and shooting skills. Hopefully, you won't show

Duffle Bag Items for Elk Hunt

✓ 6 pairs of socks   ✓ wool jacket

✓ 3 pairs of wool socks   ✓ down vest

✓ full change of clothes   ✓ rain slicker

✓ long johns   ✓ sweater/sweatshirt

✓ leather hiking boots   ✓ neckerchief

✓ wool cap with ear flaps   ✓ camera

✓ 3 pairs of gloves   ✓ binocs

✓ winter pac boots with extra liners

When preparing for an elk hunt, it is advantageous to list individual items. Lists help alleviate the chore of packing by reminding hunters to pack the necessities. For example, this list was created for packing a duffle bag.

up in a new pair of leather hiking boots that have never been worn. Likewise, don't show up with a rifle you do not intimately and comfortably know.

There is a seemingly endless flood of information and statistics about which rifle caliber and bullet combination is best for elk. Remember, it's not the thunder that kills; it's the lightning!

Bull elk can carry a lot of lead. You must hit one in the heart or lungs or you will probably lose him no matter what you're shooting. A .30-06 or .270 or even an old .30-30 with iron sights in the hands of a disciplined, skilled hunter will produce more meat than a .475 with a rangefinder 10X scope in the hands of a "dude." So, throughout the summer and early fall, do a lot of shooting. Know where your rifle shoots at various distances up to 400 yards. Then, when your guide tells you the elk's distance, you'll be more prepared for the shot. One of the mistakes made by hunters who are unfamiliar with the terrain is overshooting the bull. They usually think the animal is farther away than the guide says it is. Another is that they don't concentrate on the shoulder. You would be amazed at how many big bull elk are shot through the antlers with rifles and bows, especially if the bull is close—say, 100 yards or less.

The vision in the hunter's mind is of this beautiful trophy on his office or den wall. The vision should and must be of the bull's shoulder. Most importantly, the hunter must see that his rifle's cross hairs are indeed firmly engaged on that shoulder. If at all possible, the hunter should always have a rest. He should take a deep breath, hold it, lean into the rest and burn those cross hairs into the shoulder while slowly squeezing the trigger.

That First Elk Hunt

I always feel sorry for the hunter on his first elk hunt. Everything is so strange and different that it's very difficult to stay focused. Prime elk country is absolutely breathtaking in more ways than one. You may find yourself gazing at a spectacular view a mile or even 50 miles away while a nice bull silently drifts his harem through the timbered slopes barely 50 yards from you.

At the higher-than-usual elevation, you will find getting into and zipping your sleeping bag can be a breathtaking experience. Also the walking is all uphill! You leave camp in the morning and it's uphill all day long. When you want to return to camp, it seems it's still uphill. How can that possibly be? Only in elk country! It's not bad enough that the uphill terrain is painfully breathtaking, but your guide is always up front sucking up what little oxygen there is in the thin air! But seriously, talk to your guide. Let him know your limitations, concerns, objectives and abilities as early in the hunt as possible. Believe me, he really wants to get you onto a big bull elk. He will probably hunt you hard—practically nonstop until about 11 a.m. Then he's ready to take a break for lunch and a nap until about 3 p.m. Sometimes, he will take you back to camp; however, usually he'll look for a place somewhat out of the weather and be sound asleep in less than five minutes. Follow his lead because he's going to expect you to be sharp and deadly during the two hours just before dark.

A good guide will only give you as much help as you need. After all, it's your hunt and you should go home with a sense of accomplishment and a warm feeling of lifelong friendships which were established with the guide, outfitter, cook and other hunters in camp.

Every elk camp and hunt is different. There are many elements to a successful elk hunt. Harvesting a large trophy-class bull produces a wide range of mixed emotions for the hunter, guide and outfitter.

One of the drawbacks of elk hunting (if it can be called a "drawback") is the breath-taking scenery. This beautiful scenery has a tendency to envelop first-time elk-country hunters, making it difficult for them to concentrate on the hunt.

Everyone's ego is boosted. The hunter, guide and outfitter are all congratulated and admired by everyone in camp, as well as neighboring camps and in town. Hunting elk in the pristine country they inhabit is a rare privilege that should not to be taken lightly; harvesting a big bull is not a frivolous experience. Regardless of what you pay for your elk hunt and whether you harvest a bull or not, it is money well spent. At the very least, you are going to enjoy a valuable learning experience about yourself and how you relate to nature and your fellow man. You will be released from the constraints of your everyday routine.

In the frosty sunrises and tranquil sunsets, you will sense an inner peace, a renewal, a self-worth. You will acquire a lifelong respect and admiration for the elk species. And, while looking upon this experience with a glow of accomplishment, there will be a moment of silent tribute to the bull for his grace, majesty and ultimate sacrifice.

7

Waterfowlers: Ask Questions First, Shoot Later
by Bill Miller

Collecting rich memories to relish when withered muscles and brittle bones no longer carry us into the marsh is one of the reasons we hunt. For every waterfowler who donned a cattail brown mackinaw and cradled a favorite scattergun while wedging a duck call between his lips, there are a thousand reminiscences of "the good old days."

Everyone cherishes thoughts of opening days with grandpa, dad teaching the difference between wood ducks and widgeon, a young dog's first retrieve and a veteran's last.

If you've been hunting for quite some time, you may have one or two memories of birds pouring in. Maybe it was a day when the mallards were drunk on Manitoba barley and all the shooting in the world wouldn't keep 'em out of the field. It could be a time that a record-setting blizzard forced bluebills to run the gauntlet until you ran out of shells or a porridge-thick fog set in and the geese thought your calling sounded better than a foghorn to a wayward mariner.

If remembering the great days is fun, then recalling the less-than-sterling days is educational. The days when you've tried everything, but failed to turn a single green head should teach the most. They help make you a better hunter in the future!

While I was growing up, my dad often equated my learning abilities with that of the Missouri mule. You know, the famous one that required an oaken 2x4 to get his attention? Well back then, I always denied the resemblance; however, as I look back now and see how long it took for the lessons that ducks tried to teach me to sink in, Dad may have been right on the money!

It was a cold, rainy Sunday afternoon on the spiralling downside of the Wisconsin duck season. While most avid Wisconsin hunters were scouting for the quickly approaching firearms deer season, NAHC Member Mike Boeselager and I arranged to meet at a popular local public hunting area.

This place was set up to be one of those pass-shooting situations around a refuge with a retrieving zone in between. In fact, the locals called the place "The Firing Line." It wasn't our favorite place or kind of duck hunting, but at least we would be out hunting instead of sitting at home wishing we were.

We arrived at almost the same time and, miracle of miracles, were the only two hunters in the small graveled parking lot. We were stunned! We did not know of anyone who had ever claimed to have this place to himself.

The firing line's inside border was the retrieving zone; the outside was privately owned cornfields. The parking area sat at the top of the L, and the best position on the line was about three-quarters of the way down the foot of the L. This small rise helped a hunter gain a few yards advantage on the usually high-flying birds.

Thrilled to be able to claim the "top spot," Mike and I hurried off down the fence line. Because guns weren't allowed in the retrieving zone, we couldn't walk diagonally across the L. Our objective, therefore, was about one-half mile from the parking area.

Not too long into our walk, we witnessed a scene through the rain and fog that started our hearts pounding! Ducks landing—flocks, pairs and singles—right at the base of the small hill where we were headed!

It was our first visit of the year to "the line." We didn't know that the drainage ditch which separated the public land from the cornfields had overflowed and flooded the corn. Any mallard would consider the result paradise. However, we probably wouldn't have seen a bird if the cold front with heavy rain hadn't ushered in a new flight of birds from Canada.

What would have normally been a 10-minute forced march turned into a 45-minute stalk! We stopped many times and laid belly-down in the wet grass waiting for more large flocks of mallards to land. More and more birds came in, and none left! Mike and I were totally transfixed by the growing flock. A long-tailed rooster pheasant flushed practically under Mike's nose during one of our belly-flops, yet we both managed to resist temptation.

Memories like this last forever in the hearts and minds of waterfowl hunters. Nothing compares to your first hunting season jump-shooting or decoying, whether it's spent with your father, grandfather or good friend.

This position is a common one to assume when waterfowl hunting. Belly stalking, as well as belly-down waiting can help you strategically place yourself for a good shot.

There were so many ducks in that flooded cornfield that their feeding chatter was a roar in our ears long before we were within shotgun range.

Even in those formative years when hunters measured success by a full game bag, Mike and I had no use for anyone who would shoot a duck on the water or upland bird on the ground. We followed our plan when we reached the tall grass near the ditch by moving about 50 yards apart. For a minute we each half-sat, half-lay at the edge of the waist-high grass, trying to bring breath and pulse under control. We were both afraid to even raise an eyebrow skyward for fear of alerting the duck flocks still piling in.

Mike held up three fingers high enough for me to see, and slowly pulled them one at a time back into his palm in a silent count. On three, we both stood up. The air filled with ducks.

True to form, Mike's side-by-side double barked twice. Two fat, orange-legged drakes folded. Also true to form, the bank on the ditch where I jumped up gave way as I brought the gun to my shoulder. My first shot went straight into the sky as I fell into the muddy water. Still stunned, I discovered my second shell was a flock shot with no result. With the third shell, I did knock down a hen which had held a little bit longer than the rest of the now-departed congregation.

We retrieved our ducks and babbled excitedly about the scene during those previous minutes. With more than three hours of shooting time left and not another hunter in sight, we had high expectations of filling out a bountiful limit under Wisconsin's point system governing duck hunting in those days.

Mike and I often reminisce about that hunt. And every time we do, we agree we blew it! In actuality, we saved a lot of ducks' lives that rainy afternoon!

That day, we never saw another duck in range, or out of range for that matter. The birds in that flight must have been shot at heavily on the trip from Canada; it only took one volley of shotgun fire to let them know what was happening! I doubt they ever crossed that refuge line again without going to altitudes that require an oxygen mask!

The fact that not a single duck returned to that webfooted smorgasbord should have been sufficient education not to be so quick on the trigger, but it wasn't.

Several seasons later, I was hunting one day primarily for ruffed grouse with my dog Cinder. I had finagled a rare opportunity to hunt during the week so I elected to cover some of my favorite spots on public land—beside great grouse covers. There were streams and sloughs in this area known to hold an occasional duck, so I took a 12 gauge loaded with steel 4s. Those loads would do a number on grouse, could be pressed into service on woodcock if needed and still would keep me legal if I did find webfooted fowl.

One slough in particular held some promise for ducks. I had been watching it for many years, and, for some reason, it held more water each season. Because this had been a particularly wet year, I thought it might make a good hiding place for a duck or two that had been chased out of nearby, popular public hunting areas. This "wet spot" was a couple ridges back from the nearest road, and dense stands of pine, hardwoods and brush surrounded it. It was on state forest land; deer hunters made drives through it every year. Even though it was spongy, the slough had always been dry enough to walk across, so I thought the few deer hunters who knew about it might give it a try for duck hunting.

I wasn't being overly serious about the search for webfoots as the dog and I approached the slough's small, open-water portion. I let the dog range in front for woodcock and grouse. Typically, the dog busted through the brush at the pond's edge and went for a swim. The alders at the slough's edge were thick, so I couldn't see the dog when she hit the open water. Without thought, I noisily pushed my way through the brush. When I did, the entire surface peeled away into a melee of squealing wood ducks and squawking mallards.

I couldn't believe they didn't flush at the sight of that little black-and-white springer swimming toward them! Now, however, there were more ducks in the air than one man should be allowed to have in range during an entire season!

Uncharacteristically, I maintained composure and shot two wood-duck drakes, followed by a mallard drake. They hit the water in evenly spaced "plops" while the other ducks continued to mill around. Cinder, never much one for the cleanup work, continued looking around on shore while I waded into the water to collect my birds. Instantly, I began planning for the next day. This was going to be great!

Knowing now about this hotspot, I was sure this would be the best duck season I had ever seen! I should have known better. When faced with such inflated confidence, ducks always seem to know just how to pop the balloon!

Early the next morning, I duplicated the previous day's approach to the pond, only this time I wore waders and kept the dog at heel. I eased slowly through the thick brush trying to be as silent as possible. When I reached the water's edge, I stuck my head through the veil of alders.

There was nothing there! Nada! Zilch!

I then stepped fully through the brush, and a lone drake mallard jumped from the pond's far side. Having fully steeled my nerves for another thunderous flush of duck scads, I promptly missed the drake three times as he kicked in the afterburners to clear the trees at the slough's end.

However, I did not lose faith—yet. I thought I arrived too early in the day; the ducks were probably still feeding. Yah, that was it!

Wrong again, Missouri Mule Miller!

Though I hunted that slough a dozen more times during the entire season at all hours of the legal shooting day, I never kicked more than a pair of ducks off it at one time! I had kept my mouth shut, and I didn't see signs of other hunters finding a "honeyhole." Therefore, the ducks weren't being chased off by hunting pressure; they just weren't coming back in any kind of numbers.

Well, as the saying goes, " ... fool me once, shame on you. Fool

A dog is a hunter's best friend both in and out of the water! This lab is retrieving a mallard for his master. Having a well-trained hunting "partner" makes a waterfowl hunt more enjoyable and efficient, whether decoying or jump-shooting.

me twice, shame on me!'' Fool me a third time, and you better take
away my shotgun! That didn't happen. I named that place ''one-time
slough'' in my hunting journal.

Following that season of frustration, I moved out of the area and
went off to become a magazine editor in the big city. However, I
never forgot about ''one-time slough.'' It was always in the back of
my mind.

About six years passed before I got the chance to go back and
hunt that place again. I worked it out so vacation would find me
''back home'' for the opener of duck season. As seems inevitable,
visiting with family and old friends ate up the opener and the second
day of the season, too. That left me with three hunting days until the
close of the first part of the Wisconsin split season.

I was told by friends and clerks at the local sporting goods stores
that hunting pressure was heavy in all the old familiar places on opening weekend. I began to think about ''one-time slough.'' Had anyone
found it yet?

On Monday morning, I hunted a tiny glacial lake that Dad and I
hunted when I was in grade school. A few ducks decoyed warily.
With a three-bird limit, I let everything that came within range fly on.
I wanted to hunt more than I wanted to take home ducks.

About mid-morning my curiosity about ''one-time slough'' peaked
I whistled in my dog Gunner who was exploring terrain new to him,
packed up the decoys and paddled to the landing. Rain had started,
hard and steady. It was a morning for nostalgia. In fact, it couldn't
have been much better.

The drive to the trailhead was short. In a few minutes, I was letting the dog out of the crate and squirming back into damp waders.
Like old times, the springer and I hunted grouse on the way in; however, on this sloppy day, the ruffs stayed hidden. It seemed like we
did less wandering than I remembered from past hunts. My steps
were drawn on a straighter course to ''one-time slough.''

With Gunner at heel, I stalked within a few feet of that one-time
flush site five seasons ago. Everything looked amazingly the same.
The brush was still thick, and a heavy fringe of cattails bordered the
pond. Not trying to be too quiet, Gunner and I busted through the
jungle.

''One-time slough'' was alive again! Mallards, wood ducks and
teal flew in every direction at once. I brought the gun to my shoulder,
found a drake wood duck and slapped the trigger. I pumped the action. In the swirl of birds I found another wood-duck drake and pulled
the trigger again. A fat drake mallard flew to my left. I swung past his

Waders are virtually a necessity for most waterfowl hunters. Chest waders provide the most "waterproof" security. Make sure to always wear a belt around the top of them (unlike this hunter). The belt prevents water from filling the waders if an unexpected dunking takes place.

bill and pulled the trigger again. I could have had my limit right there! Yes, you read that right—*could have*!

Three unfired shells lay in the bottom of my pocket. A few minutes earlier they had been in my gun. I removed them from the chamber and magazine during our approach to the slough. Temptation might have gotten the better of me if I had not taken that precaution; I wasn't going to be fooled again.

Gunner swam around confused; there wasn't anything to fetch. I carefully waded across the open water to a leafy blowdown on the far bank. It was a perfect perch for the springer and me. It hid us well at the pond's edge and even broke some of the rain-laden wind. I sat down on the trunk and Gunner sat close by shivering with excitement. I felt tremors of anticipation, too!

From deep inside my waders, I pulled out a damp handkerchief to wipe the rain from my glasses. Then I pulled the camo hat further down over my eyes and popped the duck call free from inside my camo coat.

Our wait was short. Within 15 minutes, the first flock of wood ducks came back in. They screamed straight down from treetop height without hesitation. They were on the water so fast, I hadn't even raised the gun.

The "O" in "okay" wasn't even fully out of my mouth when Gunner leapt for the small flock just a few yards away. The birds took flight again and one steel 4 took a richly plumed drake at 15 steps. He collapsed on the water, and Gunner swam to him and brought the bird back.

Another flock of woodies came in practically drafting on the wind sheer of the first. This time I was ready. Another drake worthy of mounting hit the water when the flock tried to land. Gunner brought him in, too.

Teal and more woodies settled in quickly and silently; they eased back out just as silently. Then after 30 minutes, four mallards appeared above the trees. A soft chuckle on the call committed them without as much as one circle. The only drake in the group joined the brace of woodies on the log.

By law we were done, so Gunner and I drifted back into the woods and sat down again. From this secluded vantage point, we watched. Within two hours the slough filled with ducks like it did when we first stalked it.

The next two mornings, I slept late, savored Mom's breakfasts and enjoyed repeat performances of waterfowl hunting the way it should be at "one-time slough." Because the first segment of the

One of the most effective methods to hunt waterfowl is flushing the birds from an open area, like a marsh or picked cornfield, then hiding in some nearby natural cover, like a deadfall or standing corn. Once you're settled, simply wait for their return.

split season would close soon and I wouldn't be back to hunt for at least a year, I let a close friend in on the secret spot. That is, of course, only after he swore on his copy of "De Shootin'est Gentman" to hunt "one-time slough" the same way I did. He reports that he and his dad had fabulous hunting right up until that little slough froze shut for winter!

The lesson finally sank in. My secret to enjoying the best waterfowl hunting, especially in these days of restricted limits and shortened seasons, is to unload my gun! Ask questions first and shoot later. I guarantee you'll enjoy it whether you take a duck or not!

8

Scrape Hunting Secrets
by Ron Doss

Stalking whitetails, the hunter spots a bathtub-sized scrape. Over-head, he notices the mangled limbs of a thick-trunked cedar, its bark stripped bare from its base to waist high. Aromatic sap still oozes from the bruised tree. Freshly overturned humus reveals to the hunter that the scrape is fairly new.

The overjoyed hunter, adrenaline pumping 110 percent, bends over and scoops up a handful of dirt. He rolls the earth around in his hand and sniffs for urine. Sweat droplets run down his nose as he fingers the tree's broken limbs. The rutting force that drove a buck to such frenzied activity awes the hunter.

Twenty feet from the scrape, the hunter sees two sizes of deer tracks stamped in the damp earth. The prints' edges are well-defined, not weathered and softened from age.

A doe watches nearby. The hunter had seen her bound off in white-flagged annoyance, but he has no interest in taking the doe. (She's not the big buck that made this scrape.) This buck is record-book material for sure. The buck's full shoulder mount could adorn the hunter's fireplace, eliciting oooooh's and aaaaah's from admiring onlookers for many years.

Our hunter finds a tree downwind 30 yards away from the scrape, the perfect spot to hang his tree stand. This hunter will most likely spend some long, cold hours in his tree stand. He'll watch this scrape so persistently that his eyes will begin watering and the surrounding tree trunks will begin swaying and slithering before his tired eyes.

He may score from this setup, but the kill will most likely be a curious, immature buck checking messages left by the area's dominant scrape-maker. Perhaps the hunter will give up his quest for a showy rack to mount over his fireplace. He may opt for meat by taking a doe or an immature male.

This story could have gone the other way. It could have followed the track of the hunter's mental imagery, with him scoring on the 3½-year-old, mature buck. When he first saw the scrape, he should have backed off and treated the area with the same respect he would a den of timber rattlers!

If the hunter was close enough to see the detail described, he was too close. Now the chances are his buck will never return to this scrape in daylight. He'll wait for the cover of night to take care of his business. Then he will likely snort at the human smells and hightail it for the county line.

Scrape Locale

The key to taking dominant rutting bucks is learning to spot likely scrape locations. Bucks prefer old, abandoned roadbeds and field or food plot borders. Ridgetops, deep draws, swamp edges and small clearings are also favorites for rutting bucks. The choice scrape locale must have a certain species and age of tree. The tree must have a certain give to the buck's hooking and rubbing; the amount varies according to the age and size of the buck.

These selected trees have limbs and branches which overhang a prospective scrape location. The buck nibbles and mouths the limbs and rubs the trunk and branches with his forehead and preorbital glands. This above-ground scent depository allows the buck's wind-borne scent messages to cover a much wider area than if left in the scrape alone.

The hooked and rubbed trees give the doe visual signals which prompt her mating instinct. By rubbing the tree, the buck deposits an emission from his forehead glands. This scent attracts sexually mature does in the area.

Train yourself to find and recognize an edge, an area where two or more types of cover, terrain or vegetation come together. An edge may be either an abrupt or subtle change. For example, an edge may be where a conifer stand adjoins a hardwood plot or an abandoned logging road or swamp border. At edges such as these, deer will stop, swivel their ears and thoroughly sniff the air currents before proceeding. The buck knows that edges, or changes in cover or terrain, are

Crosswind Approach And Setup

In a crosswind approach, a buck (or hot doe) will typically pause 20 to 50 yards away from the scrape, observe and sniff the air for several minutes before coming into the scrape. Nos. 2 and 3 represent the best tree-stand positions for hunters in this situation; Nos. 1 and 4 are positions to avoid.

In order to find your trophy buck during rutting season, you must be able to locate scrapes. Big bucks prefer areas where two types of terrain, cover or vegetation come together. This is an area where bucks may leave scrapes.

Mulie bucks leave their scents on tree trunks. During rutting season, bucks rub trunks and branches with their foreheads and preorbital glands, leaving above-the-ground messages for sexually mature does.

places where moving deer stop to sense-check their surroundings. For a buck stringing out a line of scrapes, what better place to put out a scent message than a spot where animals naturally pause and check their surroundings?

When proficient at recognizing these likely places, seek them out when scouting and still-hunting. Watch closely for hooked or rubbed trees—the bigger the better. Stop often when in or near edge or change areas and glass the surroundings. Be sure to check for the tell-tale blazes made by a prerut or rutting buck. Look closely for dis-turbed or broken branches or an inordinate number of leaves on the ground. The leaves will be in disarray, not lying smoothly as from normal leaf fall. If your binoculars do not show this level of detail, invest in a high-power, lightweight monocular. Find one that is shirt-pocket size or collapsible. With this secondary glass, you can spot the scrape itself from rifle-scope distance.

Don't get so involved in looking for rutting sign that you ignore that big, black eye near a distant log, or the one peering at you from a downed treetop. Look for the distinctive glare and movement of antlers, too. More than once I have found the scrape-maker while setting out to scrape hunt!

It is not safe to use a rifle scope to glass surroundings while combining hunting and scouting. The strong temptation is to use the glass mounted on your rifle. I've found myself staring into an eye that had a blaze orange cap just above it. Bring the rifle's scope into play only after you have positively identified a legal target. Then, don't hesitate! Bucks don't grow highly visible racks by posing for hunters! If you've sighted the buck you want, you have to be ready to take him— quickly.

A licensed, 1½-year-old pet buck has a pen to himself. The enclosure was once a cattle feedlot, giving a sense of the area and space he inhabits. Though he's the dominant buck in his area, even if by default, he's never made a scrape. He has no contact with other deer, only human beings.

"Buckwheat" may be an exception to the millions of deer in the wild, but I strongly suspect from experience that scrape-making is reactive. Until a doe triggers the buck's scraping instinct, he will merely hook or rub trees. He deposits scent from his forehead, pre-orbital and oral glands on the visual displays of the hooked trees. It is the subsequent pheromone release in does that triggers the buck's scrape-making instinct. A lone buck will not make scrapes.

Active And Inactive Scrapes
Although you've read of territorial scrapes, impulsive scrapes, line scrapes and even doe scrapes, there are, for our purposes, only two kinds of scrapes: active and inactive.

Whitetails are not territorial. That may come as a surprise, but it is true. Bucks inhabit a preferred core area, usually selected when they were driven off by their pre-estrous mothers. This driving away of male offspring as they become sexually mature prevents inbreeding. If a second-year fawn is seen in the company of a doe long after August or September, you can bet that the tag-along is a female. The males are gone by that time.

This core area is not, in the true sense, a territory. More than one mature buck can inhabit a core area. They may even bed down side by side. When the rutting urges begin, however, they become isolated and aggressive. This aggression is stimulated by the proximity of a willing doe—not territory.

Even hastily made scrapes have a purpose. Imagine a string of

When glassing for rutting sign, you need to observe various details that may indicate scrape territory. If this is not possible with binoculars, invest in a high-powered, light-weight monocular that is small or collapsible.

scrapes along a ridge, around the edges of a swamp or following an edge. Picture them as a fisherman's line, set with baited hooks at different locations and fished until one or two of the hooks gets enough bites to establish a pattern of catching fish. That is exactly what a string of scrapes is intended to do: "Fish" for does.

Early on, the buck smells does from direct contact or from tracks with residual interdigital scent or spots where does have urinated or deposited fecal mass. That screams "doe" to his brain! This direct or indirect contact with does triggers the scrape-making instinct.

The buck, through this minimal contact, determines from the minute scent residue the age, sex, general physical condition and probable estrous onset of the doe or does. The scent kicks off his role in the annual reproductive cycle. He sets out his "line." Early in the season, he checks the line scrapes sporadically. The season progresses. His own internal functions and glandular secretions thicken his neck, broaden his nose and swell his tarsal glands. Now, he checks his scrape line more often, looking for a "bite."

A doe begins to sense or "feel" the nearing onset of her estrus and leaves a urinal or fecal message in one of the line scrapes. She may also rub her forehead gland on one of his nearby hooked trees, or lick the bared inner wood to reinforce the message. The buck checks his line, interprets the complicated messages and goes into frenzied activity.

He bares the ground, scraping and flinging the accumulated leaves and ground cover, digging his nose into the scent-soaked earth to catch as much scent as possible. He will "phlemen" the scent by curling his lip to trap and concentrate the scent, then inhale it, forcing the scent deep into his nostrils. To him, it must be like an inter-nasal shot of mating drug. It saturates his nasal membranes, going directly to the correct sensors in the buck's brain. He is in full rut. The line scrape is now an active rutting scrape.

Depending upon the urgency of the doe's estrous onset, she may lie down nearby and wait for the buck to return and find her. When he does, she leads him in a merry chase, sometimes for several days. They may romp over miles until she senses the exact moment that copulation will accomplish impregnation.

The buck may stay with her after this first act for another few hours, insuring his bloodline's continuation by several more toppings. Then the impregnated doe and the fathering buck go their separate and disinterested ways, not meeting again except by chance encounter.

Let's return to the point in the reproduction cycle where the buck finds the doe's message in the scrape. If our hunter happened on the scrape before the buck's return and went through the antics described, the story ends there. The buck will usually abandon a contaminated scrape entirely, despite the doe's urgent message. The buck's self-preservation comes first. He must stay alive if he is to pass on his genes to another generation. He may work the other scrapes on his line, but chances are he will abandon the area altogether and start over again with a new scrape line somewhere else. If the buck is spooked enough, he may go to the next county or township before settling down to his scrape-line routine again.

Treat a rutting scrape like the biggest timber rattler in the world. Stay away from it. Examine it from a long distance with binoculars. If you are unable to assess the scrape's condition at that distance, climb a tree to get a better angle or point of view. Make sure that the tree is downwind of the scrape and far enough away from any approach or exit trails into or from the scrape.

Does leave urinal or fecal messages in line scrapes. Bucks, such as this mulie, will phlemen the scent. They curl their lips to trap and concentrate the scent, then inhale it deep into their nostrils.

Wear trapper's gloves—the elbow length neoprene/rubber kind —and rubber boots or rubber-bottomed pacs when scouting, examining scrape areas or entering and leaving the hunting area. If possible, wear a neoprene rainsuit, too. Leather, cloth, human skin, sweat droplets and even your breath can leave scent deposits that will send the B&C buck snorting into the next state, leaving a dead scrape.

Don't make the fatal mistake of thinking "cover" scents will mask human scent, making the "keep your distance" edict inapplicable. Most cover scents are made from carnivores' (meat-eaters') urine. The cover scent alone is enough to alert the deer. Man may be the only predator left that regularly preys on whitetails; however, somewhere in the deepest recesses of its brain, the deer knows it's a prey animal, and the presence of a meat-eater means danger. If a cover scent is used, the smell may invoke a mental image in the deer of a man riding a huge red fox or coyote that urinates a lot! He'll still distinguish your scent. He'll know you have been, or still are, in the area. Forget skunk scents if you have any social ambitions. They linger—through baths, showers or scrub-washes!

I began experimenting with scents in the early '60s. I found a natural sour-apple candy. In everything I read about deer hunting, the statement that "deer love apples" was presented as a fact. The candies smelled and tasted exactly like green, unripened apples. Some friends and I tried them out on deer that inhabited a 30,000-acre hunting club. Many of the deer on the club land lived and died of old age without ever coming into contact with humans.

We traveled to a remote area of the club property where roads dwindled into trails and then vanished. We knew this area was seldom visited by club members, caretakers or any human beings in general. We theorized this area would be a perfect control area in which to try the candy on isolated deer.

We placed a piece of candy, moistened in nearby branch water and stored in cellophane, in the middle of a well-used deer trail. We were careful not to impart any human scent to the candy. The trail led from a bedding area to a field-pea plot. The peas were in full pod; the deer were tearing them up, foraging on the sweet peas inside. We hid within view of the candy "bait" that lay on the trail and waited.

A 10-point buck ambled down the trail toward the pea field, seemingly unconcerned, until he neared the candy. He assumed an aggressive posture, ears laid back and the hair on his back bristling. He sidled—the only word to describe his gait and motion—toward the candy in the trail. He kicked at it carefully with a forefoot. He

When examining scrape areas, hunters should wear elbow-length neoprene/rubber trapper's gloves. If possible, they should wear rubber boots or a full-length rainsuit. Any type of human scent deposit will usually result in a dead scrape.

sniffed it, inhaling the strange aroma deeply. Then, he snorted in alarm, raised his flag to full-flight height and abandoned the area posthaste. We could hear the deer feeding in the pea field repeating his snorts. Then we heard their hoofbeats as they, too, lit out for parts unknown.

The candy may have had an ingredient, other than the natural apple scent, that spooked the buck. The ''natural apple flavors'' noted on the candy wrapper may or may not have been completely natural. We may have contaminated the candy with our own scent, despite our care. Assuming the best scenario, though, this deer had never smelled an apple before. He encountered something unfamiliar and definitely out of place in his habitat. The best action or reaction of a prey animal that is controlled by instinct and conditioned is to flee the unknown—he did just that.

Seems to me that commercial scent-makers are either missing the point, or they are in cahoots with the deer. The production and sale of carnivores' urines as cover scents is logically counterproductive to successful deer hunting. Cover scents made from the urine of raccoon or opossum, or other widespread, non-threatening omnivores or vegetarian species would appear to have a much wider, more effective application than carnivore urine.

Another incident involving natural scents took place at a camp near Enid Dam in north-central Mississippi. Our camp was a travel trailer that was set up in a pasture. The pasture owner ran goats. Each morning when we left the pasture to go to stands or to still-hunt, we made it a point to walk through and cover our boots in the freshest goat droppings we could find. Billies, the male goats, have a forehead gland that exudes the foulest smelling scent. (Far worse than the most odoriferous catfish bait known to man). We'd rub a billy's head with our gloved hands and spread as much of the foul-smelling scent on our clothes as we could stand. At night, the clothes and boots were removed outside the trailer and placed in a tight-lidded locker a comfortable distance away and downwind from the trailer.

When we hunt this camp, we still go through the goat ritual. It must work. Our success ratio in this heavily hunted area, most of which is bounded by or on public land, is very high compared to others who hunt the area. Soaked from head to foot in goat scent, I've had deer come close enough to touch.

These deer are accustomed to smelling human beings in their woods. Loggers, farmers, the pasture owner and forest service and state wildlife agents regularly patrol the area, often on foot. The goat smell may not completely mask our human scent, but it apparently subdues it enough not to spook the deer during hunting season. To complete the circle, the deer we spooked 25 years ago with the apple scent might spook just as readily at a whiff of the goat scent, if that scent were unfamiliar to him.

Recently, during a muzzleloader hunt, my son, Chris, took a mature eight-pointer; it weighed just over 180 pounds. For that area, where the average kill is a spike or button averaging 13 months in age, it undoubtedly must have been the dominant buck. Chris shot from about 90 yards while the deer worked a scrape. He noticed the deer when he saw the clouds of humus flying through the air and heard the buck grunting. Enthralled with what he saw, Chris waited for the buck to complete its scrape and work over the overhanging limbs. He finally put the buck down with a spine shot as it was hooking a tree adjacent to the newly made scrape. Chris was stationed quartering crosswind from the deer. Any errant wind gust could have carried Chris' scent to the deer. However, Chris had gone through the goat-

The best scent when hunting deer is "no scent." Commercially-made scents are sometimes counterproductive. It's best to find a product that eliminates human scent instead of covering it up.

scent ritual before going out that morning, apparently proving its effectiveness once again.

Pay attention to your hunting surroundings. In the immediate area, wild grapes may be bearing or chunky ripe persimmon berries may be falling to the ground. Crushed and used for "masking"—not "cover"—scent, these natural-to-the-area smells may give you the tiny edge in time to take that big scrape-maker. A road-kill raccoon found on the way into the hunting area may provide enough musk for that necessary edge, too.

Think. Be observant and creative, and never assume you will cover your scent entirely. Masking it with natural-to-the-area scents is one way to go. However, commercially made scent shields have proven effective for eliminating human scent.

If stand-hunting from a fixed or climbing stand is your forte, select as least four stand sites—again, rifle-scope distance from the scrape. Four sites will be necessary to assure a downwind standing site. The prevailing wind, the opposing wind after frontal passage, and the other two transitional wind directions between the prevailing and frontal winds must be reckoned with. If the scrape is unhuntable from all, or any, of the four wind directions, select a stand site, or sites, downwind of an approach or exit trail, keeping the same distance from the trail as you would from the scrape.

The last day of the season, I took a 3½-year-old eight-pointer weighing 209 pounds. He was working a scrape. I was at a distance of 167 yards and used a 7mm-08 loaded with 74 grains of 4350 behind a Hornady 139-grain Spirepoint. I rejected earlier chances at three smaller scrape inspectors. Examining the downed deer was the only time that I got closer than the shot's distance to the scrape.

Locating and studying scrapes requires experience and the use of extreme caution. You need to treat scrapes like dens of rattlesnakes. Once a scrape is located, analyze it from a distance. To prevent human scent from contaminating the scrape, the wind direction needs to be considered. If it isn't and human scent is in the air, the buck that made the scrape will be long gone. If you treat a scrape with respect and don't grow impatient, you most likely will be rewarded with a mounted rack.

9

Improved Wingshooting
With Right Shotgun
by Bill Hanus

Everything I needed to know about wingshooting I learned from Rex Gage, the former chief instructor at the Holland & Holland Shooting School near London, England. Gage told me, "Bill, when you're on, you're on. When you're not, you're not."

Amen!

Since then, I've devoted a big part of my life to getting myself and others "on" with a shotgun.

"On" means being able to consistently hit the target you're aiming at whether it's feathered, furred or molded of clay. Many have preceded me in this challenge and, undoubtedly, many more will follow. We've all taken divergent paths.

For example, I look at some of the concoctions that trap shooters carry to the firing line today and see very little connection between their equipment or style and field shooting. On the other hand, the handicap trap shooter, who has been ingrained with "space gun" mentality, would have difficulty achieving his goals with the shotguns and shooting techniques I advocate.

Therefore, the key to successful wingshooting is to find what works best for your shooting situations and practice that technique until it becomes second-nature. Then you've got the right gun and the right style.

In making this gallant quest, don't be a gun snob! To do so is to defeat yourself before you start! Maintaining an open mind and a willingness to try something new certainly should improve your field wingshooting capability.

A big part of the story you are about to read is my search for perfection in a hunting shotgun. You'll no doubt disagree with some points. That's good! However, keep an open mind and be willing to adapt what is said to your own wingshooting. I think you'll find much of the information useful!

Searching For The Perfect Birdgun

I am proud to say a line of shotguns called the "Bill Hanus Birdgun" exists today. It is manufactured in Spain by Ugartechea S.A. and imported by Precision Sports of Cortland, New York. This line of side-by-side shotguns is the result of my long personal search for the perfect hunting shotgun. Several hunters seem to agree with my selection of certain attributes because the number of BHBs sold each year increases.

The Bill Hanus Birdgun story begins in the 1960s, with the merging of the Ithaca Gun Company and the then little-known, 100-year-old Japanese gunmaker SKB. For a brief moment in history, this talented combination produced a complete line of shotguns, including pumps, semi-autos and over/unders. The most notable, though, was a super side-by-side double gun!

This corporate deal benefited everyone. Ithaca's double-gun expertise was teamed with SKB's state-of-the-art technology and craftsmanship. I fell in love with the Ithaca/SKB doubles and spread the word through *The SKB Newsletter*, a support newsletter for similarly afflicted wingshooters.

The Ithaca/SKB double's shooting qualities attracted favorable notice by others, including Don Zutz. In his benchmark book, *The Double Shotgun*, he referred to the Ithaca/SKB as one of the best production shotguns in the world. He specifically recommended Models 280 and 480 because their straight grip/semi-beavertail configuration "puts the palms of the hands in the same plane."

Outdoor writer Jerry Warrington began searching for a "perfect double," also. He started with an Ithaca/SKB Model 200, 20-gauge, 28-inch modified/full double and worked with gunsmithing experts David Catchpole and Nick Makinson.

To maintain the integrity of the chrome-lined bores, Makinson milled the muzzle-end of the barrels, reducing the choke from m/f to a loose improved cylinder/modified.

Catchpole replaced the pistol grip with a straight grip and straightened the trigger guard. He then slimmed down and refinished

To be a successful wingshooter you need to find the technique that produces the best results. Then, practice it over and over again. And remember, always keep an open mind!

the wood with a hand-rubbed oil finish, recheckered it and capped it with a Silvers' leather-covered English pad.

I felt privileged to shoot this gun and was absolutely thrilled with its qualities.

The consulting team of Bill Hanus Birdgun designers expanded significantly after adding Parker-Hale of England and Ignacio Ugartechea, S.A. of Spain. In the early 1970s, Parker-Hale searched for a good double to go with its fine line of high-power and African-game bolt-action rifles. Ugartechea, a double-gun manufacturer since 1922, had a sleek, lightweight Anson-Deeley boxlock with middle-gauge guns built on frames proportionate to the gauge. Ugartechea also practiced the European method of setting each buttstock with cast-off, benefiting the right-handed shooter.

All the key elements had fallen into place for Bill Hanus' dream gun: palms of the hands in the same plane, open chokes, frame proportionate to the gauge and cast-off.

Greg Pogson, sales manager of Precision Sports, the U.S. importer for the Parker-Hale doubles line, shook hands on the deal. The first 20 Bill Hanus Birdguns in 16 gauge were delivered in 1989.

Today, the Bill Hanus Birdgun comes in three gauges. Each gauge has its own frame size, with weight proportionate to gauge: 16 gauge —6½ pounds; 20 gauge—6 pounds; 28 gauge—5½ pounds. Standard features include straight grip, semi-beavertail forend, single non-selective trigger, case colored receiver with English-style engraving, factory-choked skeet 1 and skeet 2, 26-inch barrels with Churchill raised and tapered rib, automatic ejectors, automatic safety, oil-finished and checkered walnut, and a lifetime operational warranty. Standard stock dimensions are 1½ x 2½ x 14¼ inches to a checkered butt with ¼-inch cast off.

Designing "On" Into A Shotgun

The Bill Hanus Birdgun line incorporates the most important features which make a shotgun "on." However, it certainly is not the only shotgun which is "on." The design attributes are the most important, and they can be found in one shape or form in many shotguns of both production and custom types.

Palms In The Same Plane. One of life's great shooting pleasures is a straight-gripped gun. As Don Zutz accurately observed, when you get the "palms of the hands in the same plane" you shoot better. When you mount a straight-gripped shotgun, your wrists automatically cue your elbows to be up and away from your sides (the proper place for them to swing left or right). A baseball player at the plate

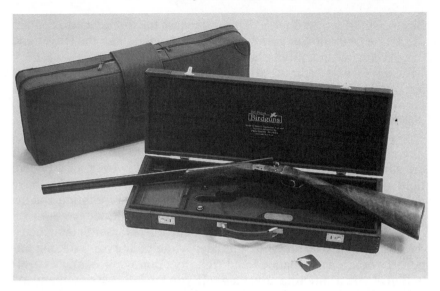

The Bill Hanus Birdgun keeps the palms of the hands in the same plane, has an open choke, frame proportionate to the gauge and cast-off. It comes in three gauges—with a special frame size for each.

proves this statement. While swinging the bat, his elbows are well extended from his body. This positioning aids his control and maintains freedom of movement.

With a straight-gripped gun, it is almost impossible for your arms to be in the wrong position. Also, it's unlikely you'd have a death grip on it to steer or cant the gun as a substitute for proper lateral upper-body movement.

Although the semi-beavertail and the splinter forends in the Ugartechea line have almost identical profiles, most American shooters would rather put their hands in boiling water than touch the barrels of a shotgun with their fingers. It is ridiculous watching a grown man trying to shoot a gun while balancing the forend on the fingertips of his left hand. The left hand plays an important role in the shooting process. The wider surface of a semi-beavertail, or the forend of a pump or auto, provides the American shooter with something to hold other than the barrels.

Major manufacturers, like Remington, Browning and others, include some straight stock offerings in their lines. They come closer to putting the shooter's hands on the same plane than models with heavy pistol grips, but not to the same degree as the double guns. Semi-autos, pumps and even over/unders cannot offer the shallow profile like the side-by-side double. This is because the forend has to contain the action or the lower barrel. Some over/unders, like the Ruger and the Beretta, are notably "shallower" than others.

Cast Counts. Almost all guns manufactured in this country, or imported specifically for the U.S. market, are cast neutral. This compromise enables right-handed and left-handed shooters to be equally disadvantaged.

Neutral cast works for target games when you mount the gun before calling the bird. You have plenty of time to tilt your head over the stock, aligning your eye with the barrel. However, in a typical field situation, like approaching a dog on point, you need to have your head erect, eyes focused on the place the dog is pointing and the gun carried safely in a ready, but unmounted, position.

When the bird flushes (or the sporting clays target is launched), the gun should come to your shoulder while your eyes track the target. If you are right-handed and right-eye dominant, some cast-off will give you a shooting advantage. If you are left-eye dominant and left-handed, you will shoot better with a gun with some cast-on.

Cast-off or cast-on led to today's design science, "ergonomics." This shotgun marksmanship principle has been accepted in England and on the Continent; however, it has been a custom-only option for wingshooters on this side of the Atlantic. Until now! Premium shotgun lines have incorporated cast into their stocks. The most notable is Beretta. Their A390 semi-auto features a spacer between the stock and the receiver which comes set for cast-off or can be flipped for cast-on.

Open Chokes. Pete Shaeffer has a sign hanging in the clubhouse of his Pioneer Point game farm in Centreville, Maryland, that simply says: "Open Chokes Kill Birds."

To finish birds that clients have only dusted on the flush, Pete uses his 28-gauge Remington 1100 skeet gun!

Most game birds shot in the U.S. today are taken at distances of 25 yards or less. Missed 40-yard birds keep flying. This is because the shooter did not allow enough lead and/or did not follow through his swing. It's the amount of lead required, not necessarily the amount of choke required, which increases proportionally as the distance to the target grows.

Prove this to yourself. Stand on station four in a skeet field. This is a 4-foot lead to break the bird over the center stake. The flight path of the target is 21 yards and at a right angle to the firing position. If you increase the distance from 21 to 25 yards, you need a 6-foot lead; at 30 yards, an 8-foot lead.

Recently, premium shotgun lines have added cast into their stocks. The Beretta A390 semi-auto is the best known model in the United States. Its spacer between stock and receiver can be flipped to cast-on.

A 50-percent increase in the distance to the target across the front requires a 100-percent increase in lead. Lead, not choke, is the critical factor. That's born out in the success of A.J. "Smoker" Smith, the world champion sporting clays shooter. Smoker uses a Winchester over/under with 31-inch barrels choked improved cylinder/improved cylinder and routinely takes 35- and 40-yard targets.

Even though screw-in chokes are popular, they cause the shooter to focus on the wrong element. The main challenge in hunting and sporting clays is to be able to shoot ahead of the bird! If you are shooting behind the bird, it doesn't make any difference what chokes you're using; the load will not make contact with the bird!

Chokes tighter than skeet 1 and skeet 2 handicap the hunter unnecessarily. Skeet 1 is a choke constriction between cylinder and improved cylinder. Skeet 2 is between improved cylinder and modified. These constrictions are perfect for upland game, for sporting clay and for steel shot.

Shot String Dynamics. The shot string is probably the least understood of shotgunning dynamics; however, it is difficult to understand lead without knowing what really happens when you fire a shotgun.

When you shoot a 12- or 20-gauge (or .410 for that matter)

shotshell, the pellets exit the barrel in a compact mass. When the lead pellets strike a target 35 yards away, the "shot string" is 12 to 14 feet long with two-thirds of the pellets in the front half of the string. When you lead a target, you should put that 12- to 14-foot-long projectile in the target's path. If you've done your job right, the target commits suicide by flying into the huge "net" of shot you've hung in the air.

Ultimately, you want the target to intercept the string's densest part, the front half. If you increase the lead, you increase the chances of this collision.

Experienced skeet shooters know how to "read the break" on a clay target and adjust the lead accordingly. The leading edge, or "beak" of the target, is called the "money side." A shooter who consistently makes the strongest hit on the target's front half will most likely take home the prize that day. Within the limits of common sense, it's difficult to over-lead. If in doubt, get out in front and keep swinging!

Gauge affects shot-string length. Two popular gauges, the 16 and the 28, have shorter shot strings. Even though the 16 gauge has fewer pellets in the air than the 12 and a 28 gauge has fewer than the 20, those smaller pellet counts are concentrated in a substantially shorter shot string. Do you remember this old saying about the 16 gauge: "It carries like a 20 and hits like a 12?" Well, it's true and now you know why!

I recommend moderate loads of the hardest shot you can buy. Look for something like 5-percent-antimony content with a nickel or copper coating in 7½s, 8s or 9s. Load the 9s in the first barrel and go for a head shot on anything that flies. Use 8s or 7½s in your long barrel. If you are working over a good dog, you'll always have 7½s and 8s left over when the season ends, providing you stay on the target's "money side."

Try The Middle Gauges

I'm hooked on the middle-gauge guns—the 16, the 20 and 28, especially the 16 and the 28. One of the best things you can do to improve your wingshooting and to get more enjoyment out of your hunting and wingshooting practice is to try the middle gauges.

In researching the Bill Hanus Birdgun, I asked *Bill Hanus Birdguns* newsletter readers for comments on the modern 16 gauge. I ran ads in *The Gun List*, too. The letters and phone calls poured in. All encouraged me to go for it! Many of the respondents simply wanted to know where to send their money to get one.

Now with several years of experience and analysis, I can tell you

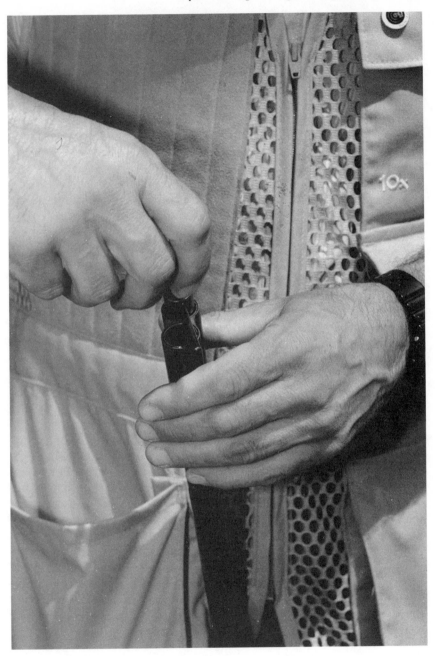

Even though changing chokes for different shots is important, it is more beneficial for shooters to learn and apply the basics like lead and swing.

that the 16 gauge constitutes about 60 percent of sales, the 28 gauge about 25 percent and the 20 gauge accounting for the balance.

In spite of the sensible, efficient "square" configuration of the 16-gauge shot string, the 16 gauge has been "bum-rapped" for too many years. There are probably two main reasons.

First, most of the commercially available loads for the 16 gauge are overloads attempting to duplicate 12-gauge loads. Second, most of the 16-gauge guns were built before 1930 when the standard 2¾-inch chamber length was adopted. The legendary "Sweet 16" Belgian-made, Browning semi-auto was chambered for 2⁹⁄₁₆-inch, 16-gauge shells. Unknown quantities of 16-gauge doubles were liberated during World War II, and virtually all of them had chambers shorter than 2¾ inches.

Even though you could insert and fire 2¾-inch shells in these guns, the results were less than satisfactory. The lips of the 2¾-inch shell never fully opened in the shorter chamber. This bottleneck effect forces the power of a 16-gauge shell through a 20-gauge opening. In such a case, chamber pressure skyrockets and recoil increases. No wonder the old 16 gauges had a reputation for kicking like proverbial mules.

Lengthening chambers to 2¾ inches is not difficult; however, in the case of the Sweet 16, the ejection port would not accommodate the fired 2¾-inch hull. The Browning chamber could be altered to fire the 2¾-inch ammo, but it would not eject the spent hulls.

These and related mechanical problems brought about the decline of the 16 gauge's popularity. Today, with a few exceptions, there is a generation of shooters missing out on the benefits of the gun "that carries like a 20 and hits like a 12."

Wingshooting with middle gauges has many benefits. For example, the 16, 20 and 28 all offer reduced recoil in hunting loads compared to the 12 gauge. This makes practice more fun and enhances the hunter's ability to stay sharp on extended shooting, such as when dove or driven-bird hunting. The middle gauges, when built into appropriately framed firearms, result in lighter, yet gracefully balanced guns which are easier to carry. That's a sure boon to every grouse and pheasant hunter who ever laced up a boot! Finally, for the wingshooter who handloads, practice is less expensive. The shot and powder saved by going to lighter loads will make a noticeable difference in the component bill over a couple of years!

Live Not By Middle Gauge Doubles Alone

Some years ago, I had the chance to shoot in a skeet league in

Gaining popularity among wingshooters are the 16- and 28-gauge skeet guns; they have shorter shot strings. This 28-gauge Remington 1100 has increased success rates for many hunters.

Albuquerque, New Mexico, using 20-gauge skeet guns in all four types of shotgun actions—pump, semi-auto, over/under and side-by-side. When the league season ended, I went over my carefully kept records to compare my performance with the different guns. (Each gun had been used equally during the league season.)

Even though I am double-devoted at heart, I shot skeet best with the semi-auto! In fact it was the only action with which I had mustered a 50 straight! I even shot the pump better than the doubles on the skeet field.

When it comes to the best combination for wingshooting under all sorts of field and range situations, I think it makes good sense to take the golf-bag approach to shotgun ownership. You need to experiment with different ideas to find out what works best for you in different shooting situations.

My Albuquerque experience helped me make some important decisions and gave me the confidence necessary to get more satisfaction out of my skeet shooting. The 20-gauge Smith & Wesson Superskeet changed my skeet-shooting life. Even with handloads, I have a career average of 96 percent with this gun. That's a bird and a half better than my over/under score. In fact, my new 28-gauge Remington 1100 skeet gun routinely tops my 20-gauge over/under average.

When wingshooting, middle gauges offer many advantages. They have less recoil, making practice sessions sharper and more comfortable. This helps if fast-paced extended shooting is required, such as when shooting mourning doves.

Some guns will simply do one job better for you than anything. That's why it pays, at least in terms of personal satisfaction, to reach into the golf bag once in awhile and see if there isn't something that will help you get more satisfaction from your shooting efforts.

When you find what works, you'll build a degree of confidence in yourself and your abilities that will, in turn, make you a better wingshot. An excellent example is a friend in California who found the right gun and is definitely "on":

Thank you, Bill, for recommending ... what has to be one of the best values I have ever procured. Barring my eventual mortal demise, for as long as I am a resident of this world, I plan never to part with my Grulla No. 2. I have owned more than my reasonable share of shotguns and have never shouldered anything that genders the level of confidence that my trusty sidelock 16 does. If it flies under 100 mph and is within 30 yards, I swear I can hit it consistently.

There are four types of shotguns: semi-auto, over/under, side-by-side and pump. When shooting in various field and range situations, it's best to take the "golf-bag" approach to owning shotguns.

Two weeks ago, I solidly dropped a 5-pound Mongolian Ringneck ... paced off at 45 steps from the point of my shot to the spot of the bird's fall ... and I'm 6 feet, 3 inches tall. My stride is about 3 feet! Can there possibly be too many things better than a fine side-by-side double, open chokes and hard shot? I think not.

Add me to your list of converts; I'm thoroughly convinced by the results. I feel unstoppable; unbeatable. YAHOO!!!!

So I must end the way I began, by quoting master wingshooting instructor Rex Gage: "*When you're on, you're on.*" No truer words have ever been spoken.

10

Backups For Dangerous Game
by Mark LaBarbera

Sometimes dangerous game force you and your guide to respond quickly with high-caliber hospitality. Handgunner Larry Kelly knows firsthand the value of a well-prepared guide. During a grizzly hunt in Alaska, Kelly planned to test special handloads in his revolver. He and his guide spotted a grizzly feeding along a river close to the tar-paper shack where they were staying. When the bear was close enough to see, and perhaps smell, the hunters, it began climbing the riverbank toward them. The guide fired two warning shots before his rifle jammed. That was like ringing the dinner bell to the grizzly!

The bear's pace quickened. Kelly and his guide began running the short distance to the shack. This wasn't the bear Kelly wanted to take, so the two men tried to avoid a confrontation. The bear didn't.

They made it to the shack and latched the door behind them, breathing a sigh of relief. While the guide worked on his jammed rifle, the party of two became a party of three.

When the bear broke through the door, it was obvious the hungry bruin intended to make a meal of these two men.

Kelly welcomed the bear with a round from his Smith & Wesson Model 29 at about 2 feet. When the .44 Magnum hit its chest, the bear roared wildly and spun around. Kelly fired again and again.

When Kelly heard the guide's gun go off, he looked quickly to see his host firing again. Kelly also shot again and again until his revolver was empty. Three adrenaline-filled bodies in that little shack was one too many.

By the time the bear died, it had taken 14 slugs. Without the guide's backup, Kelly probably would have been killed by the hungry grizzly.

Dangerous-Game Handguns

Kelly has taken big bears with the .44 and some with only one well-placed shot; however, he admits that this caliber is not the best choice for dangerous game. It would be less likely to bring down an angry bruin with factory loads than with special ammunition that handgun experts, such as Kelly, use.

There was a time when everyone, including guides, wanted to carry the .44 Magnum. But it is no longer the most powerful handgun, and it is certainly not the first choice among bear guides for a backup gun.

Instead, the .454 Casull from Freedom Arms captures the most attention from bear guides who carry handguns. This single-action revolver produces about twice as much energy at the muzzle as does the .44 Magnum with standard loads. Each Casull also delivers more energy at 200 yards than the 240-grain, .44 Magnum factory loads deliver at the muzzle. After shooting this "hand cannon" with Jim Morey of Freedom Arms at the North American Hunting Club Jamboree in Las Vegas, I would recommend that any guide who wants to become proficient enough with it to save his life should start with light loads before working up to "bear busters."

According to Hal Swiggett of the Outstanding American Handgunner Awards Foundation, most of the Alaskan guides who are using the .454 Casull are reloading their ammunition with a little extra kick.

Guides who use handguns for backup say that they're compact and easy to carry. They are most effective when fired at close range on unsuspecting game. Though it's true that a bear or lion will most likely be at close range, rarely will the animal be "unsuspecting."

Once a bear sees you, hears the muzzle blast or feels the first bullet, its adrenaline starts pumping, giving it life after death. That extra energy might be all that's needed to close the gap between the bear, you and your guide.

A guide wants to protect you and protect himself, so he's going to carry plenty of firepower. Though the handgun is compact and certain models have a romantic appeal, the majority of guides feel safer with their favorite long gun. They know that they're dealing with the

Grizzlies are powerful animals. They require a lot of firepower to go down—and stay down. Guides prefer large-caliber rifles or shotguns when backing-up hunters for these unpredictable and dangerous animals.

For guides who carry handguns, the .454 Casull packs quite a punch. Backup handguns are most effective when fired at close range.

king of the food chain. This ferocious animal fears nothing and will eat anything.

The Best Backup Gun

As hunting gun expert Bill Miller of Minneapolis, Minnesota, says, the best backup gun is the one your guide never has to use. Guides certainly don't like them, but there are times when confrontations with dangerous game are unavoidable.

When I was leopard hunting with Gary Baldwin of Hippo Valley Safaris in Zimbabwe, Africa, I saw the reluctant look in his eyes when at dark he had to look for my cat. He didn't know whether the leopard was dead, alive or somewhere in between the two. He found it—dead—but I'll never forget his face; it said plainly that this was not the best part of his job. Baldwin usually carries his pet European side-by-side rifle with open sights and 18-inch barrels. However, when he has to trail dangerous game he switches to a double-barrel shotgun. He loads this 12-gauge backup with buckshot for "close encounters of the furred kind."

Alaskan outfitter Rocky Morgan of Kodiak Island says that his favorite backup gun is a 12-gauge pump shotgun with slug barrel and slugs.

Another Alaskan-brown-bear guide uses a 12 gauge made from stainless steel. The marine models offered by American gunmakers stand up to harsh elements, particularly moisture from rain, snow and saltwater. This particular guide replaced the wood stock with a Pachmayr handgun grip and added a sling so he could carry the gun across his back, leaving his hands free for glassing or skinning. That way, his backup gun is always within reach.

Other guides were split on whether a backup gun, no matter what style or caliber, should have a sling. It's nice to have a sling for ease of carrying the gun, many said, but that piece of nylon or leather can get tangled on your pack frame, brush and other things. Outfitter Ron Fleming of Smithers, British Columbia, said, "When you need your backup, you need it now!"

In the Hunter's Information Series book *Hunting North America's Big Bear*, a guide and two hunters approached a moose carcass where a grizzly was feeding. All three men had .300 Win. Mags. When they were about 50 yards from the putrid moose remains, the bear brought its head up and stared at the hunters. Despite being surrounded by the stench of dead moose and being that far from the guide and his clients, the grizzly identified human scent. It tested the air to confirm that intruders were moving in on its meal.

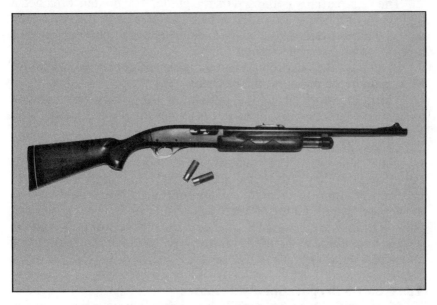

A favorite backup in heavy cover is the short-barreled shotgun loaded alternately with slugs and buckshot. This setup has prevented dangerous situations from occurring.

Whispering, the guide directed the hunters to shoot the big grizzly. One hunter froze; the other quickly found a rest. The bear perked up just before the hunter fired. When the hunter unleashed the .300 Win. Mag., the grizzly was blown off the log.

As the bear struggled to regain its balance, the guide yelled at that same hunter to shoot again. The second shot hit the bear's left leg. It came running at the guide and the hunters.

The first hunter shot again and again until the firing pin clicked on an empty chamber. The guide and now the other hunter opened fire. The guide put his first shot into the bear's chest. The other hunter emptied his gun. The bear stumbled briefly but kept on charging. The hunters scattered. The guide fired again just as the bear was about to reach him.

A nearby tree briefly provided refuge as the guide ducked behind it. But the bear was on him in a flash, slashing the guide with his claws and knocking the backup gun from his desperate grasp. A powerful blow put the guide down. The bear sunk its teeth into the guide's arm and then bit off the man's scalp.

Suddenly, from only 10 feet away, the two hunters fired, knowing they had to risk such a dangerous shot because, if they didn't, the guide would die for sure.

The bear partially collapsed on the guide. The hunters breathed a quick sigh of relief, much as Larry Kelly and his guide did when they closed the cabin door in the bear's face. Then the clients helped their host out from under the animal.

Suddenly, the bear roared and struggled to get up. A .300 Win. Mag. slug to the brain put the bear down for good.

The guide survived and still talks about the grizzly bear that took at least five bullets to the head and neck before giving him an "Old West haircut."

Guides and African professional hunters try to save themselves from such situations. They take time with their clients to sight in rifles. Covertly, they also check out a hunter's shooting ability. Lives may depend upon an accurate and appropriate rifle and load, and on the shooter's skill. Guides want to know your limitations before you pull the trigger. But no matter what you're using or how good you are with it, your guide will cling to his own backup gun like a young child clings to a security blanket.

The Guide's Preparation And Advice

If you understand what really happens when your bullet hits an animal, you'll know why a guide equips himself the way he does.

Before a guide ventures out with a client on a dangerous-game hunt, the guide will observe and determine the client's shooting ability. Time is taken for sighting in because lives depend on the firearm's accuracy, the proper load and the shooter's skill.

He'll insist that both of you be loaded with the knockdown power you need for dangerous game.

Leopards are tough, but lions and North America's big bears are even more tenacious.

In a guide's dream world, you would place your bullet perfectly and down the cat or bear with a brain or spine shot. Unless you're in tight quarters, however, the brain is a tough target because of its size. Even if you're in tight quarters, the meat-eater will most likely be moving toward you, and your nerves might have you moving, too.

In the real world, hunters sometimes hit the liver or major arteries. Although these shots can be deadly, they are not necessarily instantaneous. In my job at North America Hunting Club, I'm in touch with hundreds of guides and outfitters, and they say that the last thing they want to do is trail a wounded grizzly or brown bear. I've heard of heart-shot grizzlies that didn't even know they were dead on their feet as they ran into thick cover. The hunter and guides didn't know for sure either, so blood trailing was an adrenaline-filled experience until they found the dead bear.

My friend Bill Love Sr. of Love Brothers & Lee in Smithers, British Columbia, instructs his grizzly hunting clients to "shoot just below the hump," referring to the bear's distinctive shoulder muscles. "That breaks the bear down so you can put another shot in it," Love says.

Guide and author J. Wayne Fears tells of guide Mark Meekin's bear encounter, illustrating Love's point:

"A hunter he was guiding became very ill, and Meekin left the sheep camp at sundown to seek medical help. As darkness approached, he was making his way down a steep mountain trail as fast as he could when he almost ran head-on into a grizzly. Startled, the bear charged.

"Meekin knew his first shot needed to be a good one. He dropped to a kneeling position and held a sight picture on the bear's shoulder just beside the head. Due to the poor light and the bear's movement, the sight picture was difficult at best. The first shot broke the shoulder, spinning the bear around. Meekin emptied his rifle as fast as he could into the thrashing bear's lung area. When the dust cleared and the bear lay still, it was only 10 yards from where Meekin was kneeling. A miss of the shoulder on that first shot could have been fatal."

Meekin, Love and most professional grizzly guides and outfitters recommend guns of .300 caliber or larger. The .338 Win. Mag. is by far the favorite caliber for inland grizzlies and brown bears. Though the .416 has received a lot of attention among hunters for big, big

Some guides may choose to use handguns as backups for dangerous game because they are compact. If handguns are used, it's best to shoot unsuspecting game at close range; however, rarely will a lion or other dangerous game be ''unsuspecting.'' Be ready for a fierce confrontation!

game, there haven't been many guides willing to give up their pet backup guns. These guides find beauty in battered stocks and delight in dented barrels; each is a battle scar worthy of its own campfire tale.

Bill Love's favorite backup gun was a .338 Browning bolt-action given to him by bowhunter Fred Bear before one of their hunts. Love said it was a pretty gun that could do the job; he nearly cried when it was destroyed in a tent fire.

According to Fears, "A few inland grizzly guides, such as Ken Kyllo of Hudson's Hope, British Columbia, said they would take a hunter who was using a .30-06 with an appropriate load, provided the hunter was very familiar and proficient with his rifle and load. But they would personally carry a .300 Win. or larger caliber.

"Larry Rivers, master guide from Talkeetna, Alaska, wants folks in his camp to use at least a .300 Win. Mag. on inland grizzlies and a .338 Win. Mag. or .375 H&H Mag. on brown bears. Cy Ford, who guides along the coast of British Columbia, is very specific. He wants his employees and hunters to use a .338 Win. Mag. with a 250-grain Nosler Partition bullet."

Bolt-actions are preferred over semi-automatic rifles by members of the Alaska Professional Hunters Association and other outfitter groups. Guides have a built-in bias against semi-autos and pumps because they believe the bolt is more reliable and less likely to fail when they need it the most. However, in all our research, we have not been able to find documented proof that this is true.

In fact, a guide will perform best with the action he feels most comfortable with. For example, when our grizzly hunting group was in the Kispiox Valley of British Columbia, guide Dave Larson carried a Marlin .444 lever-action, Daniel Boone VIII (a direct descendant) used a Browning BAR semi-auto in .30-06 caliber and the outfitter had a bolt-action 7mm Wthby Mag. As we sat around the campfire, we learned that none of the rifle actions had ever failed its owner. Dave told us about how he had been saved years before by the quick lever-action, because he was able to shoot repeatedly from the hip when an injured grizzly stood up 15 feet away from him. The bear had been laying low, waiting for its pursuers.

On that trip. Daniel took one of the biggest black bears I've ever seen, and he did it with two quick shots when the bear sneaked up on our frail wilderness spike camp.

Ron "The Guide" Young of Corpus Christi, Texas, who has booked hundreds of hunters for dangerous game with guides in Africa and North America, recommends that his clients put as much emphasis on the selection of their riflescopes as on their rifles. But he

NAHC Member Larry Frisoli took this 10-foot, 4-inch Alaskan brown bear in the Alaskan Peninsula. He used a .375 H&H Mag., Winchester Model 70 with 300-grain bullets.

makes the point that guides should stick to open sights.

"Low-power scopes, including variable power models up to about 7X, are fine for hunters," he says. "I place added emphasis on reliability and weather resistance. On the other hand, I've never met a guide for dangerous game that felt comfortable chancing a scope foul-up on his gun. Open sights are the norm. A guide can't afford to waste time getting on target."

Unfortunately, I neglected his advice about low-magnification scopes while on an African safari because it was easier to leave the 3X-to-9X Redfield Widefield on the gun. The scope was reliable and weatherproof. It had helped me take a nice eland at long range one morning, but that same afternoon it almost cost me dearly.

As we rounded a bend in the trail, we came face to face with a lion. I shouldered the .375, peered through the scope and discovered that it was still on 9X! The lion's head, mane and part of the chest filled the scope. Those piercing yellow eyes were big as could be.

I aimed and fired for that part of the chest visible below the lion's chin. It wheeled around and roared loud enough to make our tracker's knees shake. A quick second shot was nearly impossible because I couldn't find the lion very easily in the scope, which was set at high power. Both shots connected. Nonetheless, the guide's backup gun had open sights, and he made two quick shots on the lion as it jumped into the bush.

After finding it, we went back to pace off the distance. The lion had been only 26 short paces from where I first shot. A half-minute later or a few steps closer and the cross hairs would have been useless.

It's experiences such as this that make a hunter and his guide happy to know a good backup gun is readily available.

11

Cropland Whitetails
by Larry L. Weishuhn

Food is a key ingredient to the welfare of any species, and white-tailed deer are certainly no exception. Agricultural areas, especially where row and field crops are grown, generally have extremely good soils and climates with good amounts of annual precipitation or irrigation. With the intensive agricultural practices utilized today, including annually fertilized growing crops, the soil's nutrient levels in these areas are further increased and improved. These agricultural practices have greatly benefited the human population, as well as the various wildlife species living in these areas.

The white-tailed deer populations have recently increased in croplands where cover remains along streambeds and occasional woodlots are found. The increased food supplies as a result of farming have created an ideal situation for producing healthy deer herds, especially large-antlered bucks. The record books prove this. For example, many huge bucks have been taken in such states as Iowa, Ohio, Indiana, Illinois, Missouri and Kansas, as well as the Canadian provinces of Saskatchewan and Alberta. Some of the bigger whitetails now come from areas which have scattered farms and croplands in states such as Texas, Georgia, Alabama and Mississippi.

White-tailed deer are extremely adaptable animals. Given a little cover and some protection, they will thrive nearly anywhere. Whitetails are not only adaptable to habitat, they can also adapt quickly to hunting pressure and practices. Bucks make rubs and scrapes in the fall. They leave tracks and droppings. Those are constants; however, the methods used to hunt them depend upon the habitat, past hunting pressure and, to some extent, the animals' wariness.

One of the most farmed areas in the Midwest lies in east-central Illinois' Piatt County along the Sangamon River. This area served as a research project of the Illinois Natural History Survey for many years. Under the guidance of Charles M. Nixon, 286 deer were captured and 96 of them (38 bucks and 58 antlerless deer) received radio collars. These deer were tracked to determine their day-to-day activities in this intensive farming area. The study's results suggested that bucks often remained in the cornfields for extended periods of time. However, Nixon also learned other important aspects. "In tracking 10 bucks that were three years old or older," he says, "we learned that they moved to open-cover buck habitats in the late summer and early fall to help protect their antler development and to increase visual interaction while they established social dominance before the breeding season.

"The range occupied by older bucks was dominated by row crops or frequently flooded bottomland forests with sparse understories. Corn and soybeans seem to be considerably less of a threat to developing antlers," he concludes.

The study area received considerable hunting pressure. Also, the study showed corn harvesting had a dramatic and consistent effect on daily and annual deer taking. If a substantial amount of corn remained standing at the end of the hunting season, the kill rate on deer was extremely low. The standing corn provided cover, and the deer would scatter in it.

The study also showed that bucks over three years old roamed large areas (normally over 1,900 acres) during the fall breeding season. However, other studies revealed individual bucks in similar farmland habitat have fall home ranges in excess of 24,000 acres.

A 1,500-acre refuge stood in the center of the Illinois study area. Interestingly, the study showed that deer did not move to the refuge in response to hunting pressure. The deer did, however, seek out more densely vegetated areas as hunting pressure increased. Or, they hid and reduced daytime activities rather than travel great distances, such as moving to the refuge. White-tailed deer, especially mature bucks, are survivors and good escape artists.

Food Plots And Cornfields

The overall wildlife management program designed to increase the size of deer within a herd and increase antler development in-

The author took this buck near a standing corn crop. The buck was moving from the standing corn to the western creek bottom.

Deer sign in standing corn crops are usually in the form of stalks knocked down, portions of the stalk eaten and, definitely, kernels missing from the cobs.

cludes large food plots, or "mini farms" with forage planted primarily for wildlife. These plots are usually planted with various legumes, (alfalfa, clovers, beans and peas) and corn. Cornfields provide food and cover during the summer and even into late fall and winter. Corn that is not harvested provides necessary fats and carbohydrates for the deer.

Hunting in standing corn can be difficult. A few years ago, while hunting in eastern Wyoming, I spent several days hunting for a buck that my outfitter, Rich Edwards, described as a "good eastern Wyoming farmland buck." I experienced the frustration of hunting the "corn forest." Some tracks revealed that the buck lived in the corn most of the time. The cornfield held all of his needs: food, cover, water (a small spring in the center of the field) and a sufficient number of does.

Rattling near the seep, the only open area in the standing corn, proved futile, even though the rut was just starting. I slowly moved across the rows, with the wind in my face, sweeping the field. The buck's tracks could be seen. A companion and I crawled into the field and dug a hole where I could hide. Then, we selectively cut cornstalks, creating shooting lanes. This provided several sightings of does, plus one young buck with six points. However, the bigger, older buck knew where I was the entire time, and, worse, he knew how to avoid me.

More and more hunting organizations and land managers are using food plots. This is called "mini-farming" and provides forage for deer throughout the year.

About midway through my hunt, I decided the best way to take the buck was to burn down the cornfield!

Instead, the guides suggested driving the field in hopes of pushing the buck through the open, previously harvested field. The drive worked, but not as we intended. The does and young buck ran near me; however, the older buck ran back toward and between the drivers, crossed about 300 yards of harvested corn and disappeared into a brushy creek bottom.

The drive had taken place at midday. That afternoon, I sat on a small rise near the creek bottom where I could still see the standing corn. About 30 minutes before dark, I saw a deer walk from the standing corn toward me. The deer's body was quite large. A hurried look through my Simmons 10X42 binoculars confirmed my suspicions. When the buck stopped about 300 yards distant, standing in the harvested corn, I squeezed the trigger. After we pushed him out of the corn and left, he had returned to his sanctuary. Late that afternoon, he left the standing corn to search for receptive does.

Deer drives are an effective way to see deer in farmland hunting areas. Unfortunately, mature bucks seldom do what we want them to do in such situations.

Driving Deer In The North

The prairie province of Saskatchewan has produced some of the world's largest white-tailed deer. As farming has moved north it has increased white-tailed deer populations and hunting opportunities, as well. A few years ago, while hunting one of the areas open to "alien" white-tailed deer hunters, I had the opportunity to experience Canadian whitetails. For the first two days, we sat in tree stands along trails near standing crops (flax) or drove the roads at a rapid speed going from one farm to another. When these methods proved unsuccessful, our guide suggested we try to drive—"push bush"—the whitetails out of the woodlots between large fields.

Our first drive proved unsuccessful on deer; however, it did work on black bear. I shot a prime-coat bear as he tried to sneak out in front of the drivers. Subsequent drives produced another beautiful black bear, and several deer sightings. Later the same day we pushed two bucks from a woodlot—one was shot. That buck broke from cover long before the drive actually got started. The other moved to the edge of the brush, laid down and waited until a driver almost stepped on him.

The second-to-last day of the hunt, we pushed a narrow creek bottom between two huge, wide-open, freshly planted wheat fields.

The drive had just started when I spotted a buck running toward the driver and me. He ran along the upper edge of the creek's bank. He had a huge body and big antlers. I could not find a rest to shoot from. With the distance still in excess of 300 yards and the buck running toward me, I squeezed a shot from an offhand shooting position. The shot missed. Hurriedly, I bolted in a second round and shot at him again, knowing he was about to dive into the creek bottom's dense brush. After the second shot, however, he turned away from the creek, ran across a narrow line of brush and broke into the huge open field. My hunting partner, Gary Machen, waited in the field and shot from a solid rest. The running buck dropped. The 25-inch-wide 10-pointer was later scored at 173 Boone and Crockett Club points. Although I missed both shots, at least I have the pleasure of knowing I had a shot at a true B&C buck. It still seems interesting that the buck ran directly toward the drivers just like the one in the Wyoming cornfield. I suspect both those bucks had been pushed before and realized there was safety behind the drivers.

Hunting Equipment

In many farming states, especially in the Midwest, the only legal firearms for hunting deer are shotguns and muzzleloaders, or archery equipment. This is primarily a matter of safety. In recent years, we have seen great advances made in hunting equipment. Shotguns with screw-in slug "chokes" and slug barrels have been improved greatly. Innovations in slugs, such as the addition of sabot slugs, have increased the relative range and accuracy of shotguns. Scopes for shotguns have increased the shooter's ability to shoot accurately. For muzzleloader hunters, the new in-line percussion rifles have greatly increased accuracy and range. The black-powder shooter has also benefited from the introduction of sabots which allow the use of conventional, expanding bullets in black-powder rifles. Technological advances in arrow shafts and bows have benefited the bowhunter, too. Bowhunters can choose to shoot extremely high-tech compound bows and equipment or return to simpler bows, such as the traditional recurves and longbows.

Interest in handgun hunting has resulted in special handgun seasons. Hopefully, in the future, some states will allow handguns in the areas where only shotguns now are allowed.

Thus, in many farming states, deer hunting is a short-range proposition: 100 yards or less with firearms; 40 yards or less with bows. Such short-range hunting requires excellent woodsmanship and lots of savvy as far as deer behavior is concerned.

Muzzleloader hunters often have longer seasons in which to hunt whitetails. Hunting near fields, such as this clover field planted for hay production, can be ideal.

Learning The Whitetail's Behavior

In recent years, the Midwest farming areas have produced many record-book and monstrous white-tailed bucks. A large percentage of these bucks are taken by bowhunters annually. Does this mean bowhunters are better hunters? Perhaps. But, in many instances, archery seasons start in early fall—well before regular firearms seasons. Those hunters who know the whitetail's behavior can take advantage of these early hunting seasons.

Whitetails are, to some extent, creatures of habit, especially bucks in the late summer and early fall. They feed in the same places, water in the same places and use the same travel routes between woodlots, bedding areas and fields. They are fairly predictable until breeding season approaches, then all patterns are altered!

However, late-summer patterns are usually in effect during most early fall archery seasons. An observant hunter can learn the habits of a buck with a minimum amount of scouting. I stress the word *mini-*

If bowhunters take the time to learn about deer behavior, they may have an excellent opportunity to take a buck like this. Normally, when archery seasons begin, bucks are still in their late-summer patterns.

mum. If you put too much pressure on a buck, even when scouting, he will most likely change his routine or leave the area.

Summer is an ideal time to scout for the fall hunting season, especially where woody habitat is limited. During this time, the deer have no particular fear of humans; they do not feel threatened by human presence. Do your summer scouting around the perimeter of fields. Look for trails coming into the crops, especially along fencelines. This area may also have shed antlers. Do not be misled by tracks indicating that the animal went under a barbed-wire fence. Bucks will crawl under a fence as often as does. Generally, they will only jump a fence when pressured. To determine when they are coming into or leaving the field, brush the trails with a branch and periodically check the trail at different hours of the day. Backtrack the trails to see where the deer are bedding. Remember not to put too much pressure on the deer.

Look for rubs and scrapes along the edge of woodlots and fields. The scrapes will appear as dished-out areas under overhanging limbs. Bucks tend to return to use the same scrapes each fall, year after year. Store all this information in a "buck journal," as well as on a topographical map of the area. This data will help you develop a successful plan when hunting season arrives. As fall approaches, spend very little time in the area you plan to hunt when the season opens. Remember that increased human activity in an area in late fall might completely alter the buck's activity. Instead, use this time to practice shooting.

Getting Permission

Most farmland is private property. It is best to get permission to hunt on a farmer's property long before the season opens. However, regardless of the date, always be certain you have permission to hunt or trespass on private property. In many areas, hunters have started paying for hunting privileges on private property. Paying for privileges helps ensure the right to hunt on uncrowded ground, and also encourages the landowner to meet the habitat needs of wildlife, especially white-tailed deer. In some areas of the Midwest, hunters have encouraged farmers to leave some crops in their fields, providing winter food. Such hunters have also persuaded farmers not to graze certain plots or clear brushy creek bottoms.

The Fall Hunting Strategy

After receiving trespassing and hunting permission, you should hunt the first few days of the season near the perimeter of the fields

Hunters should take advantage of natural cover and rests when hunting around crop-land. This hunter is using a fence as a rest, as well as using the brush to his advantage.

and along trails leading into them. One of the biggest bodied and most massive antlered bucks I have shot was taken on the edge of a huge green field in Michigan. Skipper Bettis, the hunt manager and my guide, suggested we hunt a permanent blind overlooking a large field which had been planted in legumes for hay and grazing. According to him, the deer started coming to the field late in the afternoon. My hunt took place in early fall shortly after the bucks had shed their velvet. This was well before the rut, and not much hunting pressure had occurred.

As the afternoon progressed and the sun sank lower and lower, does and fawns began feeding into the fields. Later, young bucks started arriving. In the trees along the edges of the field, we could see big-bodied, large-antlered bucks gathering along the fenceline.

It was not until the sun had set that the mature bucks entered into the field. It was nearly the end of legal shooting hours when the buck we were after finally showed himself. Although he fed our way,

Once the season gets underway, hunters should utilize trails leading to crops that are 50 to 100 yards or more away from the edge of the field. This tactic has proven successful time after time.

coming quickly, it seemed like an eternity for him to cut the distance to 175 yards. When he did, I centered my handgun scope on his shoulder and squeezed the trigger on my Thompson/Center Contender frame with its .309 JDJ barrel. The nine-pointer weighed 300 pounds liveweight and his antlers grossed just shy of 150 Boone and Crockett Club points.

Visiting later that night, Skipper told me, "We generally hunt from permanent blinds right on the edge of the fields the first few hunts. Then, as the season progresses we move back into the woods along trails leading to the fields. We noticed how the bigger bucks stayed back in the timber during the afternoon. It seems the longer we hunt, the farther back in the woods they stay, waiting until dark to enter the fields." I was quite familiar with this buck behavior from watching bucks on several ranches I managed. In talking to J. Wayne Fears, a wildlife biologist and hunting partner from Alabama, I found it was a behavior he knew, too. Incidentally, Fears sparked my interest in hunting "beanfield" bucks in the Southeast.

Hunting Beanfields

My first Southeastern "beanfield" buck came after 13 days of hard hunting. During that time, I sat on numerous soybean fields, clover fields and even a couple of other crops in the legume family I could not identify. Success finally came while hunting with Realtree's Bill Jordan in Georgia. The property Bill leased for hunting is primarily used for timber production, a crop in its own right. Thankfully, the landowners also have a great interest in deer, turkey and quail. As a result, they plant large fields in crops, providing winter and summer forage and seeds.

The first afternoon while hunting on a green field, I spotted several does feeding on the edge of the field. However, it was well after sundown before other deer began feeding their way into the field— much too late to identify their sexes or sizes. The same thing hap-

Green fields near standing corn are ideal places to hunt white-tailed deer. Large-antlered bucks frequent these areas in the fall.

pened the second afternoon on a different field; however, I saw considerably more deer.

The third afternoon, following some hasty scouting with some fellow hunters, a tripod was set up for me in the woods along a trail. This tripod allowed me to see the field and what looked like a "staging" area for deer waiting until dark before entering the field. Such areas are often ideal to ambush mature bucks: Locate a heavily used trail coming into a field, then move 50 to 100 or more yards away from the field's edge to set up a tree stand, tripod or a natural blind.

That afternoon I saw many different deer—more than I had ever seen before in the Southeast. The sun was just about gone when I saw a buck walk hurriedly through the woods on his way to the field. Several minutes later, he entered it a long way from where I was sitting. Even with my Simmons Whitetail Classic variable cranked all the way to 10 power, the buck still looked small in the scope. But, knowing exactly where the Browning Stainless A-Bolt chambered in a .280 Rem. was sighted in and where it would strike the target, even at extremely long distances, I decided to shoot. Despite taking a firm, solid rest, I saw my first shot miss; the second connected.

Livestock Farmland

Cropland and farmland are often associated with livestock grazing. Some crops are planted primarily for grazing, or they are harvested and then grazed. Others, such as wheat, are grazed and then harvested later. Livestock grazing pressure can alter deer movement patterns.

My largest non-typical white-tailed buck was taken on the Doudle Creek Ranch near Brownwood, Texas. The ranch operator plants various crops in several large fields each year, primarily for grazing cattle and for hay crops. My guide on the hunt, Chuck Dalchau, knew I wanted to take a monstrous eight-point buck that had been seen with some regularity on the ranch.

The field the buck had been using earlier in the season was now open to cattle. The first afternoon, we sat on a little hill overlooking the field. We noticed that the deer stayed away when the cattle were on the field. We did, however, see the buck in an open, grassy pasture a long way away from the green field. The following evening, we hunted him on the grassy plains beyond the cropland.

Before setting up, we chased the cattle away from the side closest to the grassy plain. Late that afternoon just before dark, the buck got up from his bed and stared at the farmland. Because there were no cattle on the side of the field closest to him, he started walking in that

In the early stages of the season, hunters should hunt along the edges of cropland. Elevated blinds are an invaluable asset at this time.

direction. I asked Chuck if he was sure the buck was the one we were after. He assured me it was a wide, tall eight-pointer with long browtines—either the one we were after, or possibly, a little bigger.

Chuck picked up a set of rattling horns and briefly meshed them together. When the buck stopped momentarily, I fired. He staggered. The second hurried shot missed, but the third one put him down.

I had always hoped to take a buck that looked bigger after the shot than before. The closer we got to this buck, the bigger he appeared. Standing beside the buck, we noticed that the big eight-pointer had a total of 24 points over 1 inch long and six others that fell just short of an inch. (Most of the points were near the base.) Farmland had come through for me one more time.

12

Camouflage: Here's What Counts
by Bill Miller

Camouflage is a means to an end for a hunter. The "end" is approaching game birds or animals as closely as possible to make a clean, one-shot kill. For hunters who use limited-range hunting tools, such as a bow, muzzleloading rifle or shotgun, it's vitally important.

Modern hunters take the "art of camouflage" seriously. A huge variety of camouflage patterns is available on the market today, and more patterns are being added every season. Some camouflage patterns, such as Cattail or Timber Ghost, are highly specialized; others, such as Realtree All-Purpose or Trebark, are meant to blend in almost anywhere.

Camouflage patterns have also found their way onto virtually every piece of equipment the hunter uses. Clothing, tree stands, day packs, guns, bows, boots, knives, tents, wristwatches—even underwear and toilet paper—can be found with camouflage patterns. Though some of these examples may be a bit extreme, they clearly show that details count.

Choosing A Camouflage Pattern

A good all-around hunting camouflage pattern works almost anywhere, but a specialized pattern might be considered "best" for a particular type of cover and/or terrain. If you are going to a sporting goods store to buy camouflage clothing, drive by your most frequently hunted area on the way. Notice the type of cover it contains and the levels of lights to darks in that cover. Also, bring some photos of your hunting area that were taken during the season. Compare the colors in your photos to the patterns in the store.

Consider the various cover you hunt and your most common hunting technique. Do you hunt exclusively from tree stands in the hardwoods from bow season to black-powder season? If so, you'll need patterns that look like leaves, branches and bark against the sky. These are terrific when viewed from below; however, they stand out like a sore thumb when viewed on the level in dark cover.

Are you exclusively a waterfowl hunter who spends the hunting season in cattail sloughs and flooded cornfields? If so, the cattail patterns will work best. However, if you hunt timber ducks you'll feel like a neon sign compared to your buddies hunkered against the trunks of pin oaks in their Mossy Oak patterns.

Most hunters, however, hunt a lot of seasons in various situations and different cover. An entire wardrobe of camouflage would be ideal, concealing hunters in almost any situation. However, few hunters can afford that luxury. Most own one, maybe two, sets of camouflage clothing, accommodating weather changes more than types of cover.

Even if you could own every camouflage pattern in the world, it would be impractical to stop and change clothing three times on a morning's turkey hunt because you moved from hardwoods to pines to open fields and back to hardwoods.

Matching the pattern specifically to cover helps to build confidence; however, it is not essential.

A few years ago, NAHC Shooting Council Advisory Council Member Larry Weishuhn invited me on a Rio Grande turkey hunt in south Texas mesquite country. Knowing full well I'm a northern Yankee born and bred, Larry arranged for a spell of 100-degree-plus heat for my three-day hunt.

For the greening mesquite terrain we hunted, Bushlan camouflage, which Larry helped design, probably would have best matched the cover. However, I chose to wear my lightest weight clothing—the Hide 'n Pine pattern.

Hunting was difficult because the gobblers were henned up and unresponsive to our calling. I did manage, however, to take my two birds over the course of the three days. For the first one, I belly-crawled as he dusted himself in a ranch road; he went down at 38 steps. The second gobbler came to my call at the very end of the last day. He surprised me in the middle of an opening near a stock tank.

The art of camouflage should be taken seriously by hunters. Blending into your surroundings is vitally important when hunting wild game. Many camo patterns exist for clothing, equipment and accessories. Notice this hunter's full camo headnet.

Hunters have a variety of camo patterns to choose from. Popular patterns include Mossy Oak (left), Cattail (middle) and Realtree (right). Most hunters cannot afford an unlimited variety of patterns; however, owning at least two different patterns can be beneficial.

I crouched behind a scrubby mesquite and called him in to 14 steps. There's no doubt the camo worked, though it's probably the last place the designer thought to use it.

A good camouflage pattern should cover your mistakes in various situations. The ones that do this best are already familiar to hunters. They include all the variations of Realtree, Trebark, Mossy Oak, Hide 'n Pine and good old woodland.

What Camouflage Should Do For You

The type or pattern of camouflage you choose will depend upon what you want the camouflage to do. Specifically what are you trying to hide from? For example, the turkey hunter has different camouflage requirements from the deer hunter. The deer hunter's requirements are different from the waterfowl hunter, and so on.

Bird hunters, particularly turkey and waterfowl hunters, must be the most concerned with color duplication. Because they develop such bright plumage for mating and other purposes, these birds obviously perceive color. Some scientists estimate that color perception in birds is 10 times greater than in human beings. In addition, birds have far greater overall visual acuity than most other animals. This, then, makes color camouflage one of the most important considerations. Though important, pattern matching is probably less critical.

Big game, on the other hand, has long been purported to see in tones of black and white. This has recently been contested, especially when considering a deer's visual acuity in the ultra-violet part of the spectrum. Until more studies are conducted or the legendary talking deer is found, it cannot be proven. However, it is known that antlered game, prairie game and mountain game all have good eyesight in low light for detecting motion and perceiving depth. Thus, when selecting a pattern for big game, the most important aspect is matching the terrain's light-to-dark ratios and the pattern's three-dimensionality.

How To Test Camouflage

Testing the efficiency of a camouflage pattern in a specific hunting situation used to be done with a Polaroid camera. The hunter would nestle into his blind or against a tree and a buddy would take his picture. In only a few minutes, they could see how the camera lens saw or, better yet, didn't see the camouflage.

Although this method still works, an even better one is now available to many serious hunters. It is the hand-held video camera. The video-cam has many advantages over the Polaroid—the biggest is that it records movement.

The purpose of camouflage is to hide the hunter as much as possible; that means hiding motion, too. Wearing any dark, muted color may be sufficient camouflage if a hunter remains perfectly still. However, that's not at all practical when you have to raise a gun or draw a bow or turn your head just to see an animal. The real test of camouflage is in its ability to hide these necessary movements.

Set the video camera on a tripod or have a buddy hold it on a potential hunting spot. Wearing your camouflage gear, walk into the scene and take your hunting position. For a minute or two try to remain entirely motionless—this is like taking a picture with the Polaroid. Then go into a routine of making all the motions that are necessary during a hunt. Raise your head, draw your bow, scan the terrain for animals, cough. Between each movement sit still for a moment to reestablish the camo's "hidden" effect.

If your partner is wearing a different camouflage motif, have him move into the same position and go through the same routine. This will give you a good comparison of how the two patterns stack up under the conditions tested.

Play the taped sessions back two ways. First watch them through the black and white viewfinder in the video camera. Though not perfect, this may be a good representation of how an animal, like a deer or elk, sees the scene. Then go home and play the tape on a high-quality color television screen. This method represents more closely how a turkey, duck or goose sees you and your setup.

The results may amaze you. They will certainly drive home the importance of eliminating any unnecessary movements while you're hidden.

Brad Harris of Lohman Game Calls, a lifelong hunter, game caller and camouflage expert, is amazed at the things video tapes reveal. Recently, on a spring turkey hunt, Brad, the Lohman pro staff hunters and I were testing a new cardboard, portable blind that Lohman manufactures. This blind is nothing more than water resistant, corrugated cardboard imprinted with the Realtree All-Purpose camouflage pattern. It folds up for ease of carrying and has two stakes to secure it.

In video taping and photographing this simple blind, the cameraman would zoom in and focus on a motionless, camouflaged hunter with his head and shoulders above the top of the blind. Then he would zoom out and pan away from the blind. In the meantime, the hunter would duck down behind the blind. Without taking his eye from the camera, the cameraman would then try to pan back to the blind and zoom back in. Often as not, he couldn't find the blind!

Watching the tape later in both color and black and white, it was absolutely amazing how that blind would literally disappear against the background as the camera zoomed out. Even the black and white photographs in this chapter give a good depiction of how well the right camo pattern blends into the background. Some hunters don't like the hassle of carrying a blind with them, especially when they're on the move hunting turkeys. However, such a blind is a great advantage, because it masks all motion from game.

To really assess a camouflage pattern's efficiency, shoot the same video test under various light and cover conditions. This will let you know how much movement you can "get away with" under different hunting conditions.

A Few Field Tricks For Better Camouflage

Avoid Gaposis. Even if you've done a great job of camouflaging yourself from head to toe, your gear's effectiveness will be reduced

In the past, most camo testing has been done with Polaroid cameras. However, with advancing technologies, today's video camera offers a whole new dimension when testing your camo's ability to blend in with surroundings. It allows you to see your movement—an important element when hunting.

by "gaps" in the camo pattern. The most common gaps are at the wrists between the bottom of a knit cuff sleeve and a glove's cuff and at the shin between boot tops and pants that ride up when bending your legs to support your turkey gun. These gaps are especially revealing if a shiny watch slips into the opening on the wrist or if you're wearing white socks. When turkey hunting on heavily pressured public hunting land, you may find that gaps can be downright dangerous. Only an irresponsible nitwit hunter would think that a white wrist scratching on a slate call looks a lot like a gobbler's head feeding.

Gaps at the wrists can be covered by dark-colored sweat bands. They cling snugly to keep that shiny wristwatch covered and, in cold weather, add another insulating layer at a point where the blood flows near the skin.

If you wear high, dark-colored socks, the effect of gaps at the boot tops is minimized. You could also tuck your pants cuffs in your boots or add stirrups to the bottoms of your pants legs. Camouflage gaiters also eliminate this problem and help prevent snow or forest debris from getting inside your boots or up inside your pants.

Other gaps to watch for include sweatshirt hoods protruding from above the collar, partially buttoned jackets or shirts revealing skin or a light-colored undergarment and short-tailed tucked shirts that gap at the belt line.

A full-length mirror rescued from the junk yard is not a sissy thing to have in hunting camp. A quick examination in front of it before heading into the woods will reveal existing or potential gaps.

Eliminate Shine. Nothing, repeat *nothing*, in your camouflage hunting gear should reflect light as a glare. That means your clothes, personal effects, such as eye glasses, your gun or bow and any additional equipment, such as boats and tree stands. Signaling mirrors work great when you're lost; however, anything on your visible gear that reflects sunlight will alert most game animals. About the only thing they see in nature that reflects light like that would be water in bright sunlight.

You can't be too extreme in your efforts to eliminate shine. Looking around a duck boat, for example, will usually reveal numerous potential sources of shine which could leave you wondering why the ducks are flaring at 100 yards. It could be sun reflecting off of worn oar locks, the cup from the top of a thermos, the brass of spent casings, an uncamouflaged gun barrel, the outboard's cowl showing from under a burlap covering or one of a hundred other tiny but significant sources of shine.

Eyeglass wearers should consider dull frames and anti-reflective coating for the lenses. A camouflage headnet also works great, if you can tolerate wearing the kind with no eye holes. Although these "mesh-bag" type headnets help prevent glass lenses from fogging, some hunters think they interfere too much with vision and shooting ability.

Use 3-D When Possible. The lights and darks in camouflage patterns are meant to simulate the effects of light cast on three-dimensional objects, such as leaves, branches and bark. The light areas in the pattern represent direct light; dark areas are shadows. A pattern that does a good job at this representation is successful; however, a true 3-D camouflage is even better.

A common example of 3-D camouflage shown in almost every war movie is when soldiers stretch camouflage netting over their helmets so they can weave in natural vegetation. This provides realistic color to match the terrain and create three-dimensionality.

Wise bowhunters will sometimes cut a bough from a conifer tree,

Portable blinds are a big asset to hunters. Although they can be a hassle to carry, they hide movement from game. (Notice how well this blind blends into the background.)

tie it to the front of the bow and trim out openings for the arrow and the sight. Then, when they are eye-to-eye with an elk on the ground, the act of raising and drawing the bow is less likely to attract the bull's attention.

Some camouflage clothing manufacturers are actually incorporating sewn-on or Velcro-attached leaf cutouts onto their garments.

Using 3-D camo can be as easy as sitting down behind the branches of a dead fall or pulling a few pine boughs down in front of you. Anything that naturally enhances your camouflage will give you an amazing boost in confidence.

Blacken Those Boots. The most common position for calling turkeys is with the hunter's back against a tree and his legs drawn up in front of him to support the shotgun. This pose naturally positions the feet back on the heels, pointing the boot soles at the incoming bird. If those soles are an unnatural, light color, they can be a warning beacon for that wary bird.

Buy boots with black soles for turkey hunting. Or, if you have a favorite old pair with light soles, spray paint them dull black and touch them up regularly.

Avoid Faded Camo. All camouflage patterns lose their effectiveness as they fade. The success of camo relies on the subtle contrasts between light and dark areas. As fabric dyes are exposed to light and laundering, they lose their vividness and tend to become closer to being monochrome. This will, in effect, make the camo pattern a solid color rather than a "pattern."

Follow the garment manufacturer's advice to prolong the vividness of the camo patterns in your hunting clothes. Don't ever try to "get one more season" out of them if they have started to fade. Your success will fade, too.

13

Scientific Shotshell Selection
by Don Zutz

Selecting the correct hunting load prior to 1925 must have been a mind-boggling experience. A study made at that time listed 4,067 different types of shotshells on the American market! In 1926, the ammo manufacturers combined their efforts to bring that tally down to about 1,750 loads. This number continued to decrease through World War II.

Once the production of sporting ammunition resumed after the end of the war in 1945, the different types of shotshells numbered in the hundreds rather than the thousands. This should have made it easier for a hunter to make decisions.

However, modern shotshells have become technically advanced systems. They are made from steel or lead, and their "stuffings" are more sophisticated than ever before.

Lead Shot

The popular turkey loads can help explain the importance of component contributions to performance. These loads are packed in 10-round boxes and have the specific job of placing an ultra-tight pattern on a target the size of the bird's head/neck area for multiple hits with bone-breaking energy. To help full- and extra-full-choked guns sling such rifle-like shot strings, modern turkey loads have two features: copper- or nickel-plated shot and a granulated plastic buffer. This helps reduce pellet deformation on firing setback and allow a

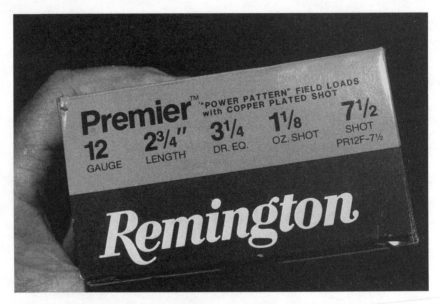

Stiff field loads with copper-plated pellets have proved successful for hunting upland birds. Patterns and hitting power increase when pellets aren't deformation prone.

fluid flow through the snug choke constriction.

Historically, the key to getting tight, energy-laden patterns has been to use shot and loading techniques which reduce pellet deformation. Deformed pellets do not fly straight and hard; they tend to flare and/or slow down upon meeting air resistance (drag), thus opening the pattern and/or lengthening the shot string, which weakens downrange performance. Plated pellets mitigate against deformation if they have hard, high-antimony lead cores. The buffer also aids against deformation by filling the voids between pellets, encasing each sphere. This prevents the sphere from flowing under firing (setback) pressures.

Buffers also allow pellets to shift about slightly within their mass while being squeezed through a tight choke. This eliminates further deformation and enhances patterning potential by establishing a smooth ejecta flow. Optimum turkey loads, then, should have hard pellets in buffer.

Which pellet size is best for turkey hunting? The No. 6 was traditional; however, reports indicate that it can fail. Pellets will deflect from rounded, feathered surfaces, and 6s can lose punch as the range increases. There is a trend toward heavier pellets, such as the No. 5s and 4s, in magnum charges, providing pattern density and pellet energy. Use 1½- and 1⅝-ounce loads of No. 5s in the standard 12; 2-ounce charges of 5s in the 3-inch 12; and either 4s or 5s in the 3½-inch 12 and magnum 10. In the 16- and 20-gauge, use the 3-inch, 1¼-ounce loads with copper-plated shot.

Dove Loads

Dove hunting consumes more shotshells than any other type of hunting. Stated another way, dove hunters miss a lot. They could improve their results, however, if they used better quality shotshells than those discount-store promotion loads. The cosmetics may be there, but manufacturers must cut costs to sell them cheaply. This is done, in part, by using very soft lead shot that deforms en masse under firing pressures. These cheap loads will usually pattern 10 to 20 percentage points below what would normally be expected from a full-choked gun.

The ideal shotshells for doves are trap loads. They have the hard-

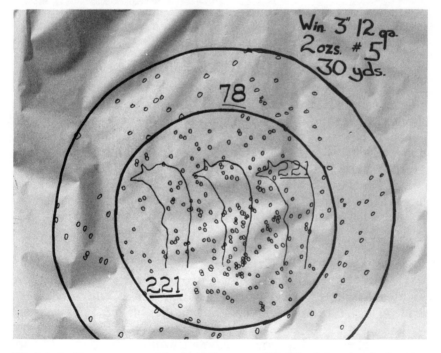

The 3-inch, 12-gauge magnum load with 2 ounces of No. 5 lead shot gives both pattern and density for turkey hunting. Also, the per-pellet energy is excellent for taking these game birds. (Left and right heads were drawn on target to show killing density exists even away from center pattern.)

Pellets with a low-antimony content, such as discount-store promotion loads, deform and weaken pattern and penetrating power. In other words, you get what you pay for.

est lead shot that is available today with about 5 to 6 percent antimonial content; thus, there will be minimal pellet deformation, meaning greater pattern density and higher pellet energy. For the 12-gauge shooter, both the 2¾- and 3-drams equivalent trap loads with 1⅛ ounces of No. 7½ shot are good choices. Remington makes a Duplex trap load with half the pellets being 7½s and the other half 8s, giving overall pattern energy plus density; it's definitely a good dove load.

In 20 gauge, Remington and Winchester make quality ⅞-ounce target loads with No. 8s for vastly improved patterning with harder pellets, but a 1-ounce, 20-gauge load is recommended with No. 7½s or 8s.

Pheasants And Prairie Grouse

Like a wounded grizzly, pheasants and the heavily boned prairie grouse (sharptails, pinnated grouse and sage grouse) can carry a lot of lead. A lot has been written about using the fine No. 7½s on these birds; however, these birds require multiple, anchoring hits from heavier pellets—unless you're shooting within the skeet's 20-yard range. Perhaps multiple hits from 7½s will shock a bird at close range when these small pellets retain some energy, but their shocking effect decreases rapidly as the distance increases. Moreover, it takes energy to drive pellets into the forward vitals and break bones on out-going shots. Hard-hitting, long-range patterns become a factor on windy days when prairie grouse flush wildly.

As an all-around pellet for moderate ranges, the No. 6 in heavy field loads is adequate. In fact, an extremely effective setup for close- and moderate-range pheasants and prairie grouse is a skeet gun or improved cylinder with 1½-ounce magnum loads of No. 6s. These particular combinations provide a broad pattern coverage with ample per-pellet energy.

However, the No. 5 is a better selection when ranges increase, splitting the difference between the energy of 4s and the density of 6s. No. 4s work well when the pattern holds tight for the longest shots. There are fewer No. 4s per load than 5s, leaving weak spots in the cluster. If No. 5s are difficult to find, it's better to use 4s than 6s for positive retrieves. Use heavy charges for pattern-filling purposes; the 1¼-ounce heavy, field load works best. Inexpensive promotion loads are anathema here, too, because of their soft shot. In order to get the best results, you should always load with plated shot or boxes marked "Hard Shot."

Quail

There are two popular quail-hunting approaches: the close-in bobwhite flushes and the farther flushes of running species in arid country. Bobwhites often have picture-book flushes, requiring only light loads of No. 7½ or 8 shot in skeet guns. However, bobwhites have been changing their habits and habitats. Those found in thickets rather than open fields should be hunted with 1⅛-ounce loads of No. 7½s for certain knockdown energy. In the 20-gauge, a good 1-ounce load is preferred; those with copper-plated No. 7½s or 8s are excellent. Winchester's 1-ounce, 28-gauge load works adequately in open patterns in this smallbore.

The running species of Western quail are difficult to find. This means you need tighter patterns and heavier pellets; copper-plated No. 7½s should be the minimum in 1⅛-ounce field loads. Some reports show that hunters who switched to field loads of No. 6s significantly improved their results, especially when chokes are tightened to modified or full. The quail is small and will pick up only a minor part of the pattern; those few hard 7½s or 6s will impact more effectively than will more hits by weaker shot. The 1- or 1⅛-ounce loads of 7½ or 6 shot are okay in the 20, but only the 1⅛-ouncer should be commonly used in the 16. Neither the 28-gauge nor the .410 is humane on far-flushing targets.

Ringneck pheasants can carry a lot of lead. Heavy field loads of No. 5 lead shot are good choices. Steel No. 3s give about the energy level of lead No. 5s.

The Winchester 1-ounce, 28-gauge loading helps fill out open patterns; however, it has a rather low velocity (1,125 fps) and should probably be used with No. 7½s as a minimum size for velocity/energy retention. The No. 6 would usually be better because it is heavier and overcomes air resistance more easily for higher downrange values.

Ruffed Grouse

Many early writers boomed No. 8s and 9s for ruffed grouse, advocating No. 7½s for the longer shots of the late season. Their thinking has influenced current writers and hunters. Although those hunting with a good retriever can use such light pellets successfully, hunters without dogs can rightly load a more potent pellet to anchor the bird for a positive retrieve. The bard of all grouse hunters, Burton L. Spiller, said it best in his classic book, *More Grouse Feathers*, ''... despite the occasional lucky shot that might prove the reverse to be true, a ruffed grouse is capable of carrying off quite a bit of lead.''

In other words, a ruffed grouse may be easily dropped; however, dropping one doesn't automatically mean a clean kill or a certain retrieve. Thus, a typical hunter should think seriously about using more knockdown energy on brier partridge.

The No. 7½ works well on ruffed grouse at close and moderate ranges, but the No. 6. works even better. Traditionalists may scoff at 6s for ruffed grouse, thinking they ruin the aesthetics of a hunt for the classic woods partridge. But what upsets a hunter's aesthetics more than a crippled and lost bird? Whether it's a 1-ounce load in the 28, a 1- or 1⅛-ouncer in the 20, or a 1⅛- or 1¼-ouncer in the 12, No. 6s have better brush-rattling ability for solid penetration on screened birds than the 7½s, 8s and 9s. The heavier 6s will drive deeper on tail-end, outgoing targets.

Quality trap loads with No. 7½s, with equally high-quality field loads of 7½s or 6s, are good choices. Copper-plated pellets aren't out of place in grouse coverts, and for a higher velocity the premium loads with 3¼ drams equivalent powder charge (1,255 fps) can be recommended. Despite traditions, the No. 8 can be a crippler and waster of ruffed grouse.

Chukars And Hungarian Partridges

Although a medium-sized bird, the chukar partridge has strong muscles, can take a hit and keep running. Modified choke and 1¼-ounce loads of No. 6s are about right. Local conditions can dictate variations, depending upon whether you are hunting in the canyons or on flatland.

Like the chukar, Hungarian partridge are runners and far-flushing birds. Unless they lie well for a dog or an approaching hunter, a tighter choke and dense patterns of No. 6s are needed. Lighter pellets like 7½s and 8s result in Hungarian partridge running on long shots, even when the hunter makes a centered hit.

Furred Game

Squirrels and rabbits, as well as hares, are popular fare for many American hunters. Many hunters underestimate the "toughness" of a squirrel's hide; many grouse hunters have failed to stop them with No. 7½s and 8s. Thus, do not take a squirrel for granted because it is small and has a fluffy, furry tail. No. 6s are about the lightest pellet seriously listed for moderate ranges; the No. 5 pellet is a better choice. The No. 4 is also effective, but it should be used in heavy loads for pattern density. A tight pattern should be used for squirrels, because they present a small target when they expose only their head/neck area around a tree trunk or stretch out flat on a high limb. Loads of 1¼ ounces are top choices, and a full choke is the best bet.

Except for open-country jacks, loads for hares and rabbits can be similar. Field loads of No. 6 do quite well on snowshoes and cottontails. The No. 5 suits all-around rabbit hunting, hitting with high energy but not causing numerous blood clots. No. 5s may be on the heavy side for many hunters; however, they do drive through bramble better than 7½s or 8s. For heavy-boned jacks, high-velocity and magnum loads of No. 4s may be needed; No. 2s in magnum doses are justified if local conditions warrant.

Steel Shot

Steel shot is entirely different from lead shot. Unfortunately,

For furred game, like tough-skinned fox and grey squirrels, a dense pattern of lead No. 5s will provide both pattern and power. Some hunters, however, prefer magnum No. 4s.

most hunters have followed their former lead-shot concepts. However, it's a new world, and the criticism heaped upon steel loads is often due to the hunter's choice of impotent pellet sizes. Steel shot, of any given size (diameter), are about 30 percent lighter than lead ones of the same size. This means that the steel pellets lose their velocity/ energy values more rapidly in air resistance, and they have more pellets per ounce.

It isn't unusual for a steel pellet to carry the same amount of energy as a lead pellet that is two sizes smaller. For example, a steel No. 4 has about the same amount of retained energy as a lead No. 6 at 35 to 40 yards, while a No. 2 steel pellet has approximately the energy of a lead No. 4. To get the energy of a lead No. 2 at 40 to 45 yards, a hunter must use the steel BB. A lead BB's energy is approximated by a steel T shot. Thus, a hunter can no longer think in terms of lead-shot energy values only.

Steel shot doesn't deform on firing setback. It gives efficient patterns, and many modified chokes will throw full-choke percentages. However, it is wrong to believe that open-choked guns will invariably print tight patterns with steel loads. Open-choked barrels (skeet, improved cylinder, skeet No. 2) will sometimes tighten their patterns with the bulkier steel pellets, such as BBs, BBBs, Ts and Fs. With the finer sizes of steel shot, such as the 1s, 2s, 3s, 4s, 5s and 6s, the open chokes will usually continue to deliver wider clusters. The improved modified choke may become one of the best all-around steel shot setups for waterfowl.

Duck Loads

When steel shot first became available, hunters chose the No. 4 because they used that number in lead-shot days. This explains the early complaints about crippling losses; steel No. 4s are not hard hitters. For all-around duck hunting, the steel No. 1 is a much better selection because of its definite penetration from 50 yards or more. Even steel BBs work for pass shooting; they give the approximate energy of lead No. 2s out to at least 50 to 55 yards. Although these large-sized pellets may seem like overkill, experience proves they kill cleanly afield.

For all-around and long-range duck shooting, the 10 and 12 gauges are necessary for optimum pattern density, because their hulls host the most shot. The 3-inch 12's 1¼-ounce load can be extremely effective with steel 2s and 1s, while also generating a high (about 1,350 to 1,365 fps) velocity level. The 10-gauge magnum's 1⅝-ounce steel load also has a published velocity above 1,300 fps. Unfortunately, the 3½-inch, 12-gauge magnum's 1¹¹⁄₁₆-ounce steel loading has a lower velocity (about 1,275 fps). The 3½-inch 12 works better for the larger steel BBBs and Ts and Fs at this velocity, because the heavier pellets retain their velocities better than 1s and 2s in the face of air resistance. There is a theory that slow steel loads are adequate because air resistance works harder and faster against a swift object than against a slow one; however, observations afield lead one to favor the higher velocities with all but the biggest steel spheres. Thus, the above charge weights are recommended over the 3-inch 12's heavier 1⅜-ounce load at 1,260 fps, and the 10-gauge magnum's 1¾-ouncer at a similar velocity with steel 1s and 2s.

For close-in gunning over decoys inside 35 to 40 yards, the No. 3 steel pellet surpasses the steel 4 as a clean killer. Steel No. 5s and 6s, even though they are listed as decoy loads, have marginal impact; they provide the energy of a lead No. 7½ when in close, and dissipating to the level of a No. 8 quickly. How many hunters ever seri-

For jump-shooting ducks, heavy pellets are needed to provide penetration on outgoing targets. The steel No. 1s and BBs are about right, although some duck hunters will have trouble adjusting to those numbers.

ously used 7½s and 8s for ducks when lead shot was legal?

For jump-shooting ducks, heavy pellets are needed to ensure deep penetration on outgoing birds. These are steel No. 1s or BBs, with an emphasis on BBs if the birds are spooky and likely to jump at long range. The 3-inch 12 with its 1¼ ounces of steel 1s or BBs is a good choice for jump-shooting.

The lesser gauges, such as the 16 and 20, are not effective for long-range gunning on waterfowl. Because of their capacity limitations, they are commercially loaded with nothing heavier than the steel No. 2, which can be a marginal pellet on geese beyond 35 to 40 yards. A full ounce of steel No. 1s or BBs will not fit a 3-inch, 20-gauge case, nor will it fit the 16's hull. These smaller gauges should be used with a full understanding of their limits.

For optimum long-range duck gunning, the 10-gauge magnum with steel BBs can be spectacular.

Goose Hunting With Steel

Geese are the big game of wingshooting, and they can absorb a lot of energy. Because such big, heavy steel pellets—BBBs, Ts and Fs—are needed to bring down geese in pass-shooting, the best loads are those which accommodate the heaviest charges, such as the

The 3-inch, 12-gauge's 1¼-ounce load with steel BBs provides the necessary penetration for the outgoing ducks taken in jump-shooting. It also works well on high mallards.

3½-inch 12 and the 10-gauge magnum. A debate still exists regarding BBBs versus Ts as the better all-around pellet. Meanwhile, the steel F-shot has come in for criticism. Experienced and observant hunters believe steel Fs are counterproductive at long range because their pattern density does not hold up over long distances, resulting in crippled and lost birds from 1-pellet hits in non-vital areas. F-shot is best inside 40 yards, because its energy gives optimum penetration and its patterns still provide multiple hits. On this basis of balancing pellet energy with pattern density, BBBs and Ts work best in magnum charges.

Gauges which throw less than 1⅛ ounces of steel must be viewed critically for geese. Even the 12-gauge's standard-length hull doesn't handle much shot in the high-speed, 1⅛-ounce loading when BBBs and Ts are involved. For the standard-length 12, steel No. 1s and BBs are needed to provide pattern density; and the hunter, of course, must discipline himself to refrain from taking skybusting shots beyond the energy of each pellet size. If a hunter thinks he must use steel BBBs or Ts in the standard-length 12, the 1¼-ounce loading should be his choice even though it has a lower velocity. The heavier pellets can compensate for this lack of muzzle velocity, and the heavier charge promises a few more pellets per pattern.

Steel Shot In The Uplands

There are already some areas, especially federal lands, on which steel shot must be used for all hunting, including upland game. This practice may spread throughout the country; therefore, steel-shot selection for the uplands deserves some forethought.

The main point is that steel pellets of any diameter carry about the energy level of lead pellets two sizes smaller. The No. 6 steel pellet, for example, has about the performance of a lead No. 7½ at close range, and a No. 8 as the range goes to 30 to 35 yards. A steel No. 5 compares with the lead No. 7 which, although not loaded today, was a truly fine upland size. And, as already mentioned, the steel No. 4 gives a downrange performance similar to a lead No. 6 when used for waterfowl hunting. Steel pellets also cut cleanly, seldom pulling the long trailers of feathers into the wound channel.

For heavy-bodied birds, such as pheasants and prairie grouse, the No. 4 steel loads can handle moderate ranges the way lead 6s did; however, when the range increases beyond 30 yards, steel 3s work best to get the impact of lead No. 5s. For long-range upland gunning on larger birds, steel 2s operate like lead No. 4s. Because there are more steel pellets per ounce compared to lead ones, the 1⅛-ounce, 12-gauge load often suffices. In the 20 gauge, a 1-ounce, 3-inch load is suggested over the ¾-ounce, standard-length loading because of its extra pellets.

For woodcock and close-flushing bobwhites, the steel No. 6 works well. Field observations indicate that steel No. 7s and 6s do not have adequate impact for positive results on the larger birds, such as pheasants, prairie grouse and even ruffed grouse.

The steel No. 5 has excellent results on ruffed grouse from open-choked guns. In 20-gauge, the 3-inch, 1-ounce charge of steel 5s can be a startlingly efficient round. When No. 5s aren't available, a conservation-minded hunter may choose to chamber steel 4s to get the ballistics of lead 6s. These larger pellet numbers may shock hunters who have always equated 7½s and 8s with the aesthetics of grouse and woodcock hunting. However, if they want clean killing power rather than crippling hits, they must learn to use them.

Steel No. 6s may not do the job on high doves. Instead, loads of steel No. 5s should be used in 1- or 1⅛-ounce charges. Far-flushing species of running quail may require steel 5s or 4s for anchoring hits.

To get the energy level of lead No. 5s for turkey hunting, use steel No. 3s. Magnum loads in this size should produce tight patterns, because steel doesn't deform. Those who want a pellet with the power of lead 4s for turkey hunting will have to use steel No. 2s in magnum doses.

For rails, the No. 5 or 6 steel load is best. Skittish Hungarian partridge may require steel 4s to carry ample energy on surprise flushes. Steel BBs and No. 1s can penetrate squirrel hides for clean kills; steel 3s and 4s are effective on rabbits and most hares. Close-in cottontails can be taken with steel No. 5s.

A Thinking Sportsman's Game

The future of successful shotgun hunting relates to making intelligent load selections on the basis of component structure and downrange ballistics rather than merely price and exterior cosmetics. Hunters need to understand the subtleties of lead-pellet harnesses and buffer and steel-shot energy values before applying them. Think beyond discount-store pricing before you select a hunting load!

14

Turkey Tactics
by John J. Woods

Turkey hunting is my passion. In fact, I'd willingly give up every other form of hunting to pursue America's greatest game bird. Since calling in my first boss gobbler in 1977 near Kirksville, Missouri, hunting this game bird has been pure addiction. It is extremely exciting facing off with one of nature's finest, knowing that your success is directly related to your own individual performance.

The fascination with turkey hunting stems from the fact that you can never become perfect at it. To consistently maintain a high success rate, you need to constantly learn new tactics and new tricks. You also need to develop an interest in learning from your mistakes afield. And that can be tough!

In turkey hunting, as in any type of hunting, success is not measured in terms of harvest tallies. The success of actively communicating with an animal in the wild makes turkey hunting unforgettable. Calling a gobbler to within range of a shotgun barrel or a camera lens is the ultimate thrill in turkey hunting.

Turkey hunters constantly strive to increase their skills and knowledge. Vast amounts of information are available to them. The problem is digesting all the data and then attempting to apply it while in the field.

Outlandish Tactics

During Mississippi's season, I had not heard an early morning gobble. About midday, I set my decoy up in a large, green field where I knew two gobblers had been gathering.

After an hour or so had passed, I noticed a great deal of verbal abuse coming from a flock of crows up the hill and toward the back of a huge pasture. I couldn't ignore it, so I abandoned my hideout to investigate the crows.

Through my binoculars, I could see 12 or more crows dipping, diving and creating havoc on the far end of the pasture. I sneaked across the pasture quickly and eased through the far side of the woods until I was within 50 yards of the crows.

I dropped to my knees to look under some pine trees. I saw one big gobbler standing 10 feet from the woods' edge in a full strut. As the crows continued their aerial attack, I counted five younger gobblers and two jakes in the bunch, too.

On hands, knees and belly, I crawled as close to the action as I could. Barely lifting my head from the terra firma, I saw that the "big boss" was gone; however, five smaller gobblers were milling around and the crows were still going at it.

I eased my shotgun forward, hoping I could shoot lying down. I had just enough saliva to eke out a low "cluck." The fivesome immediately turned in my direction and began marching in a single file—parade style—right in front of me. I clucked again, offering myself the choice of five clear shots. I chose the biggest one and collected a 17-pound tom with a 5-inch beard.

Don Shipp, an Arkansas boy who won an Arkansas State Turkey Calling Championship, enjoys copying the gobbler-drumming effect. Call manufacturer Will Primos of Jackson, Mississippi, also uses this tactic. Both hunters use extreme caution with considerable thought toward hunting safety.

Copying a gobbler's drumming sounds is designed to make a local, dominant gobbler think another bird has invaded his territory. The dominant bird will come in to challenge the suitor that is trying to woo hens away. This is an extremely effective tactic.

Kelly Cooper, a turkey-call manufacturer, concentrates his turkey hunting on Eastern species, but he says, "All turkeys gobble the same." He uses a technique called "float calling." Once the gobbler is actively gobbling, Cooper moves around on it. "I move around, about 10 yards at a time," he says, "right, left, back, until I know the gobbler is getting close. I sit down and set up at the very last possible second."

While continuing to move quietly, you should be looking for a place to settle, and, at the same time, listening intently for responses

Author John J. Woods has loved the sport of turkey hunting since 1977. In order to be successful, a turkey hunter needs to constantly learn new tactics and tricks.

Will Primos, a call manufacturer and hunter from Jackson, Mississippi, uses the gobbler-drummer tactic. This technique is effective, but requires extreme caution.

coming from the gobbler. Cooper considers this one of the most pro-active and unusual turkey hunting tactics.

Gerry Blair, a turkey magazine editor and author of a book on turkey hunting, uses a tactic that makes the gobbler think a hen has left to find better action. "I use this on hung-up toms," Blair says. "I leave the gunner in place and sneak away from the turkey yelping forlornly as I go. This gets a tom moving when nothing else will."

Tommy Bourne and David Davis from Prentiss, Mississippi, use a tactic that multiplies the common strategy of double calling. Not only do both hunters set up on the same gobbling bird, but each handles two calls. Tommy uses a mouth call and a box; David uses a different type of mouth call and a slate. This creates a hen-calling orchestra, and, boy, does it work!

Several years ago, I had the chance to go hunting with the quad-calling duo. At first light, we had six distinctly different gobblers sounding off. We chose a bird roosting directly ahead of us on an old logging road. About 100 yards into the woods, the road forked. The three of us set up right in the fork of the road.

The gobbler gave us his all from the roost, until a fly-down call from Tommy brought the gobbler to earth. With all four calls cranked up in a wild mixture of cadence and rhythm, the gobbler began a forced march directly to our position. However, a pack of coyotes jumped into the action and got the gobbler before we did.

George Mayfield, owner of a turkey-hunting guide service in Aliceville, Alabama, has a turkey-hunting philosophy he calls "getting green." It is not a hunting strategy, tactic or trick but more of a way of thinking.

Getting green means becoming one with the turkey's nature and blending into the turkey's environment. It's more than camouflaging your body to match the local, seasonal terrain. It's "knowing" the terrain and the land's layout.

George's ability to predict gobbler movement and to be able to

The famous turkey-calling duo, Tommy Bourne and David Davis from Prentise, Mississippi, execute a tactic that creates a hen-calling orchestra. Each handles two calls effectively and the results are amazing!

head off that bird by using the land's layout contributes to his over-whelming success.

Getting green develops a hunter's ability to move in on a bird without bumping him. There are risks, of course, and you may spook a few, but you'll also sneak right into the front yards of a lot of gobbling fools.

Buster Faidley, a four-time Tennessee Open Turkey Calling Champ, a two-time Tennessee State Calling Champ and a finalist in the Grand Nationals, has a "hot to trot" technique. "I get the turkey fired up," he says, "then, run away from him as far as 150 to 200 yards. I'll stop to get him gobbling again and to come in my direction, then move away a second time, establishing a path I want the gobbler to follow.

"If the gobbler continues to respond," he says, "I may repeat this action several times. Finally, I'll get the gobbler cranked up one more time, then shut up. I quickly move back toward the gobbler and the path I have established. Then, I move quietly into a position that gives me maximum visibility and shooting options."

This technique makes the gobbler so anxious to catch a hen leaving the area that he goes gobbling crazy and mindless. When he runs in, you're ready to give him a grand welcome.

When All Else Fails

Most turkey hunters have been in situations where all the tricks in the bag were used and that stubborn, ole tom is still out of gun range.

For a really stubborn tom, Don Shipp has a special plan. He spends an entire day observing and copying the gobbler's behavior. During this observational period, Don searches for the gobbler's strutting zone, a place where the gobbler struts his stuff daily. Don watches where the gobbler goes off the roost. Then, he swings around him, watching the gobbler's choice of direction. This may not always be a productive venture, but it's a way to determine where you should be when the gobbler comes along the following day.

Another trick to use on stubborn toms is aggressive calling tactics. Aggressive calling is becoming more popular every year; however, George Mayfield has been using this strategy for years with great success. "The more sexually excited I can get a gobbler," he says, "the better my chances of keeping that bird gobbling actively. That's the key to bringing him in close."

The louder and stronger a tom gobbles, the louder and stronger George returns his response. (And his responses are immediate, practically stepping right on the tom's gobbling.) "I like to bring

Turkey guide George Mayfield, from Aliceville, Alabama, is known for his "Getting Green" tactic. This tactic is more than camouflaging physical attributes; it is actually a way of thinking and requires hunters to become one with nature and the turkey.

Another good tactic is to find a tom's strutting zone and watch how the tom struts his stuff. The next day, he will most likely strut with the same pattern and direction—use it to your advantage!

some pressure to the situation," George comments, "and take control myself."

Primos often uses a common tactic that is used in the fall of the year. If he can't break a gobbler from his harem, he will jump in the flock himself. This effectively scatters the flock in every direction.

"If you can get in the right position at the right time," Primos says, "and bust them up as you would a flock in the fall, separating him from his hens is a sure way to get him to come to your calling." Every turkey hunter's greatest competition in the field is the other hens. If you can't lure the tom away from the real thing, then maybe it's time to break up the party.

A tactic I use when all else fails is a modified end-around technique. When a gobbler sees me, he usually heads off in the opposite direction after losing interest in my poor calling.

When I sense a move is in progress, I jump up and try to get around in front of the retreating gobbler. This is most often easier said than done. I do not know how a slow-stepping (but constantly moving) tom can beat me running over a stretch of turf, but it happens more often than not. If I head him off, I set up again and watch for him to pass me or try calling again.

Making It Safe

Turkey hunters need to be cautious and aware of other hunters who may be operating in the same woods.

Blair, using a defensive hunting posture, makes sure that no other hunter is in his area or working the same bird. If he sees another hunter, he announces his presence loudly and abandons that particular turkey. Blair also avoids hunting birds that are near any type of roadway, because other hunters will most likely be in the same area.

Using a turkey decoy is a popular tactic; however, Cooper thinks they only invite trouble. If you use a decoy, be extremely careful.

Cooper commented that the greatest turkey hunting danger is a hunter who "has to kill a bird." Trying to be successful at any sport can create pressures that cloud good judgment and the use of common safety practices.

Pennsylvania requires hunters to wear 250 square inches of hunter orange for fall hunting and 100 inches for spring hunting. It is only required when the hunter is moving in the woods. (It can be removed once the hunter is in position.)

Don Shipp of Arkansas recommends using at least an orange bird bag or cover when transporting a dead turkey from the woods. Some hunters put an orange band around their setup tree. I often clip a foot square piece of orange material to a nearby bush with a clothespin.

Will Primos gives this advice on turkey hunting safety: "I always do my utmost to identify my target. The people who are involved in accidents are the ones who think that it will never happen to them.

"Remember to slow down when you enter the turkey woods," he continues. "You are leaving your world of hustle and bustle. The turkey has nowhere to go, except to take care of his own basic needs for that day; he is not in a hurry. Take your time and you will be more successful and safer."

Buster Faidley says, "The biggest turkey hunting safety violation is two hunting partners separating while hunting the same gobbler. When the hunters separate, they can easily lose communication with each other even if they are only 40 or 50 yards apart.

"When they separate, they lose track of time and distance," he continues. "When one hunter moves without the knowledge of the other, an accident can easily occur."

While turkey hunting on privately leased lands with George Mayfield, I set up on a gobbling turkey near a trespassing poacher two mornings in a row. The poachers had slipped into "our" woods ahead of us and were already in position. It is a spooky situation to see another human form rise up in the predawn light and run off. In one case, we were no farther than 25 yards from the other hunter!

The point is never become complacent about a particular tract of woods you might be hunting. Even though your goal is concentrating on the pursuit of a wild turkey, you need to keep all your senses tuned in to everything that is happening in the woods.

Safe turkey hunting, like any hunting, means to positively identify your target before shooting. You should keep your gun safety on until the final second. And, finally, you should practice safe firearm handling while afield.

Remember that when you're turkey hunting, you're in the woods dressed in full camo, making the calls of a female turkey. It is too easy for the hunter to turn into the hunted. That's why it is your responsibility to hunt safely at all times.

15

Scouting
by Tony Caligiuri

Someone, not too long ago, published an article in a major sporting magazine about record-book big-game animals. Among other things, the author reached the conclusion that the majority of hunters who put their names in the record books rely more on luck than on skill. At first I was taken back a bit, but the more I pondered his arguments the more I agreed. However, luck can be helped along with proper planning, research and scouting techniques. If you're not in an area that holds game, all the rabbits' feet and horseshoes in the world won't help.

With the advent of practices such as license drawings, and big-game management by units within states rather than by entire states, these research and scouting methods have changed greatly in the last 20 years. Hunting has become more specialized; scouting has become more precise and refined. Many accepted scouting rituals have been disproved and many new methods have been added. The rise in popularity in scrape hunting and deer and elk calling have added more fuel to the fire. Some animals are more susceptible to scouting than others, but there is not one North American big-game animal that cannot be scouted. During the past five years, I have harvested 10 record-class, big-game animals. Two were taken by pure luck (both were whitetails), three were a combination of luck and scouting and five were animals that were located prior to the season and hunted as individual trophies once the season opened.

Most animals will stay within a given range. Like human beings, they desire the basic elements of food, water and shelter. Many require protective overviews where they can see, hear or smell approaching predators, yet escape if there is need. Some big-game animals require two homes: one for summer, one for winter. The hunting season often takes place during an animal's migration from its summer to winter home. In some species, like the caribou, the trip is quite pronounced. In others, it may be a slight downward change in elevation or a short move to denser timber. Because of these transitions and habitat changes, scouting methods can vary greatly depending upon the species.

My expertise in big-game hunting relies heavily on preseason scouting and research. I am not in great shape; I don't have above-average eyesight, and I don't have a substantial bank account to engage a top-notch outfitter for every hunt. Yet, because of diligent research and scouting, I feel extremely confident on every hunt. That confidence, combined with scouting knowledge, usually brings successful results.

Start At Home

Hunting should start at the kitchen table. Sometimes I let the luck of the draw determine my fall hunting plans; sometimes I'm interested in a particular species and start from there. I never plan on taking two good, representative animals of different species on the same hunt. In today's hunting environment, it just isn't practical, and it's difficult enough to scout for one species, let alone two.

Sometimes a hunter will be limited to where he hunts; therefore, he is limited to where he scouts. Others may focus on a particular state and hunt as non-residents. Then, there is always the hunter who wants a particular trophy, such as a big buck mule deer or bull elk, but doesn't have a clue where to find it. Regardless of the situation, the actual scouting begins at home before the season opens.

The first step in scouting is deciding which big-game animal to pursue. In some areas, mule deer may be cyclic, and hunting them during the down periods can be extremely difficult. Conversely, many Western states have experienced an explosion in elk populations. If you live on a farm and want to hunt whitetails, much of your scouting work has already been done. However, if you are less fortunate, then you must first focus on your quarry, then start the research.

Many writers and self-proclaimed experts suggest looking in the record books for good areas to hunt particular game animals. Even

This B&C desert bighorn sheep, taken by author Tony Caligiuri, was scouted four months prior to the season-opener! Various scouting techniques should be utilized throughout the year—not just during the season.

though the record books are interesting, they offer little value as a prescouting tool, in my opinion. The entries are usually at least three years old, and many of the hunting areas listed are off-limits to the average hunter. For example, the record book states that the biggest pronghorns come from Arizona. However, getting a pronghorn permit in Arizona may take a lifetime. Also, many of the areas that produced record-book trophies have changed drastically. In other words, you must use more current information.

As a North American Hunting Club Member, you have a valuable resource within easy reach. Articles on where game can be found are featured in every issue of its magazine, and the Swap Hunt and Hunting Reports segments of the Keeping Track section can put you in touch with other Members interested in the same type of hunting. In fact, the first place I turn to in every issue is the ''Member Shots'' section. I get a quick overview of trophies from across the country and when I see a particular specimen that perks my curiosity,

NAHC Members need to research to find the best areas to hunt. The best information is the most current information. The North American Hunter *magazine is a great way to find up-to-date information on various subjects. The Keeping Track section and Member Photos section help Members who are looking for some answers.*

I'll file it away and check future issues for repeats from the same area. If that particular area continues to look promising, I'll drop that Member a note in care of the Club requesting additional information. Most Members are happy to answer such requests.

Specialty organizations are also an excellent source for up-to-date reports. The publications for the Rocky Mountain Elk Foundation and the Foundation for North American Wild Sheep are filled with current reports on the best hunting across the country, and each lists the member's name and hometown at the end of each report. With these basic tools, and a little help from directory assistance, it's fairly easy to narrow the hunting area down to two or three states.

Once a couple of states have been chosen, the letter-writing campaign begins. I ask for harvest figures, game surveys, license drawing odds and public land access information. Then, I choose an area that has a combination of good license drawing odds, good success rates and access. This information is put into the home computer via a simple spreadsheet program. After that, all the information I need is at my fingertips. This might seem like a lot of work for the person who just likes to buy a tag and go hunting, but believe me, the payoff is tenfold.

Entry Tags
The downside of applying for limited entry tags is the short time span between the tag drawing and the start of the season; however, the tags are usually for an area small enough to be adequately scouted in a couple of weekends. Many hunters purchased tags that were valid statewide. This added a new dimension to scouting; however, statewide tags are a management practice of the past. Hunters looking for a quality "do-it-yourself" hunt, should draw a tag in a limited entry area; it makes the scouting process a lot easier. If I can't hunt in a limited entry area, I like to limit my actual scouting area to no more than 25 square miles. Of course, once I locate a particular animal or group of animals, I can bring that area down to just a couple of square miles or even a few acres, depending upon the animal and time of year. Limiting the scouting area to a key 5-mile by 5-mile area is the first important step. Narrowing down an area to 25 square miles can sometimes be accomplished without ever going into the hunting area. The first resource that I explore is people.

People who have hunted the area previously can often give you a good idea where the game concentrate. State game biologists can also be helpful, as well as forest service personnel and game wardens. However, don't expect to get top-notch information from all of these sources. In fact, while I have gotten some good general information from biologists, I've never gotten anything specific enough to be useful. I've also found that most game wardens are tight-lipped about their particular territories. I realize that other writers claim them to be a great source of information, but I have found that you have to be good friends with one before he'll give you anything that's even remotely useful.

If I do not get good information from personal contacts, I drive into the area for an initial survey. People who work at gas stations or restaurants will often open up after they've seen you a few times—they can be great sources of information. I know one hunter who struck up a conversation with a helicopter mechanic while waiting to go on a tour flight over the Grand Canyon. The conversation resulted in some useful information on where to find late-season bulls in the area where the hunter held a tag.

If I can't get my scouting area down to my 5x5 area from talking

A great scouting tactic prior to hunting season is flying over the area. Hunters get the chance to thoroughly look at the country's terrain and strategically plan their hunt.

to locals and other hunters, it's time for some leg work or, if possible, a flyover of the general area.

Flyovers And Topo Maps

One of the best preliminary scouting techniques is the flyover. In many cases, especially those involving sheep, the airplane has been abused as a hunting tool. This has prompted many game departments to institute "no hunting days" immediately after such flights. Locating an individual animal during a flyover, then landing nearby and hunting him is not only illegal, it's revolting. This is definitely not the type of flyover that is outlined here.

To be legal and ethical, the flyover should be conducted well before the season starts. Herd animals can be observed from the air if you don't harass or disturb them. You should be looking for elements that are conducive to a game animal's presence, such as terrain, cover and water. Observing the locations of seldom-used roads, landmarks and points of reference, such as power lines, elevation points (for glassing) and small out-of-the-way water holes (especially in dry years) can also be useful. When possible, mark these elements on a map. I've developed a method for doing this which has been proven to work.

I use topographical maps published by the U.S. Department of the Interior's Geological Survey (Denver, Colorado 80225 or Reston, Virginia 22092). The 1:24,000 scale is readable and adequate. For the most part, I've found these maps to be quite accurate. I like to cut the maps into potential hunting sections. Those 12-by-12-inch sections are backed with mat board or cardboard. When the targeted state is divided into game management units, as is Arizona, I'll keep the entire unit in a three-ring binder or manila folder. I never laminate maps because I like to write notes on them and mark the water areas and places where I've seen game. I find this technique to be very advantageous and successful.

Herd animals, such as this antelope, are among the easiest animals to scout. Look for sign and other variables—not just the animal. This helps sharpen scouting skills.

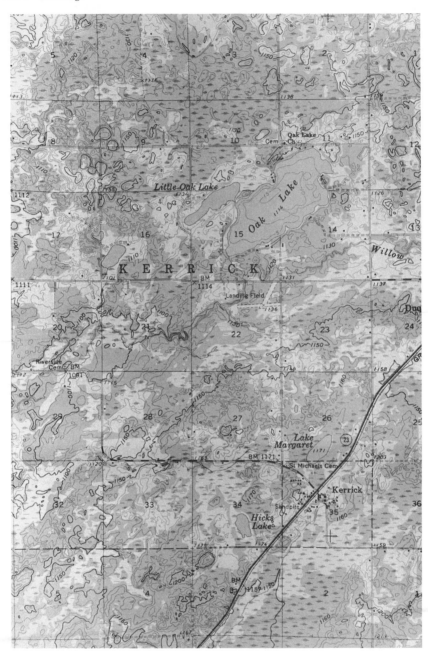

One tool that is a definite necessity for scouting is a topographical map. A topo map shows various features—both natural and man-made—in detail.

The combination of observations made during the flyover and map notes usually gives a good idea of what could have been found on the ground, but it saves a lot of footwork and time!

Area Survey By Vehicle

After a flyover, a survey of the area should be made by vehicle. In many wilderness areas, vehicles are not practical or legal. The hunter needs to rely on other methods of access. In most cases, a truck can cover a lot of hunting ground. I'm not advocating hunting from a truck or shooting out the window, but the truth is that a good vehicle is an important part of scouting.

For instance, I have several friends who plan do-it-yourself elk hunts in Colorado and New Mexico each year—most of the time with little or no success. They scout every morning at daylight and come in at dark. They climb mountains, glass canyons and generally wear themselves out before the season even opens. Most significant, however, is that even with all this work, they seldom see a bull! I did the same thing on my first two elk hunts; then I planned a trip with hunters who seldom scouted on foot and never got up before noon. They weren't lazy or drinkers, they just scouted after 4 in the afternoon and well into the night.

If this sounds a bit on the left side of the game laws, keep in mind that there is neither a gun nor a spotlight in the vehicle. You simply start driving the roads from late afternoon until one or two o'clock in the morning a week before the season begins. Elk are nocturnal animals, and you'll often see them crossing the road or feeding within viewing distance from the road. During your nocturnal scouting in the early part of the season, it's wise to stop the truck every quarter mile and listen for a bugle. Once you locate individual bulls, then you can move into the area before daylight in order to evaluate them for trophy status.

Good signs, such as tracks and droppings, can be spotted from the road. Rub trees and wallows can also be readily seen from the truck. My favorite example is a single elk track that outfitter Larry Heathington spotted in the road ditch on a dusty September day in northern Arizona. The next morning, he and I followed the track direction and set up to bugle before daylight. The bull answered and began working his way toward us. Unfortunately, he walked past another hunter who killed him. Still, we located him from a single roadside track, and he wasn't an average bull elk. He was a new blackpowder world record! (The bull is displayed at a muzzloading magazine's office headquarters.)

Shed antlers and pick-ups can give clues to the quality of game in an area. However, these types of sign will not give the exact locations.

The Field

When you've covered as much as you can from the road, it's time to move into the field and look for game. Several generations of writers have taught us that we need to look for food such as serviceberry, acorns, juniper and even sagebrush. Food sources are needed to hold game, but they are not always the best indicators. Water is a good indicator, but it's more important in dry years than wet. Many hunters assume that shed antlers mean animals with antlers. However, many animals shed their antlers on ranges quite different from their fall stomping grounds. To locate resident game in the block of acreage that has been selected as the primary hunting area takes some diligent leg work and lots of binocular time. This is when the aspect of scouting changes from mental exercise to physical exercise.

Elevation is critical when glassing. Find a high place where you can cover a lot of ground. Bruce Sitko, a highly successful guide, refers to this as primary glassing. Primary glassing is done from vantage points that encompass fields of view within 25 square miles. It shows you groups of animals only. You most likely won't be able to evaluate trophy quality or determine if they are male or female; however, a good vantage point with lots of elevation should be the first place to start.

Most outfitters say that a good vantage point is the quickest and most productive way to find out what might be in a particular vicin-

One of the most basic scouting techniques is glassing with binoculars or spotting scopes. When glassing the countryside, it is best to be at a high vantage point. This allows you to cover a bigger area.

ity. Glassing techniques seem to vary from region to region. The first time he ever hunted desert sheep, Jim Babala, the dean of modern Alberta bighorn outfitters, was amazed at the number of Arizona guides who used spotting scopes for primary glassing. Conversely, I have heard several Arizona guides say that Alaskan and Yukon guides rely almost exclusively on binoculars for primary glassing. At any rate, if you are not used to squinting through a spotting scope all day, try binoculars.

Glassing is most effective when animals are moving at dusk and dawn; unfortunately, that's when the light is at its worse. Take advantage of the sun, keeping it to your back to maximize any available light. When glassing in the morning and evening, always pay close attention to the moon. Animals start moving earlier and stay out later during certain phases of the moon. This is often the reason deer may be found at dawn during a scouting trip, only to disappear when the season opens two weeks later.

When you are glassing during the day and looking into the sun, try to find a niche to drop down into that will provide some shade.

Recently, there has been a trend toward higher magnifications for general-purpose hunting binoculars. In my opinion, next to a pair of boots, binoculars are the most personalized piece of equipment that a hunter might own. Buy the absolute best that you can afford. If that means dropping down in power to get better quality optics, do it. If you're not convinced, try a simple test. Borrow a pair of quality 8X30 or 7X40 glasses and a pair of cheap 10X40 or 10X50 glasses. Step out on the front porch with the first set, focus on a car's license plates or a street sign at 300 yards. The letters will be more readable with the quality, lower-power glasses.

Once an animal is located, you can move in closer for a more detailed evaluation. This is where the more traditional scouting methods, such as reading sign, comes into play. For all practical purposes, the scouting is over once the prey has been found. It's now time to start planning the hunting strategy. Planning the strategy will be easier because you should be more familiar with the area, and, more importantly, you'll have the confidence to be successful.

Building Confidence

The confidence that scouting brings is an extremely important part of the hunt. I once had the chance to hunt for northern whitetails with a group of skilled and experienced black-powder hunters. My friend, Toby Bridges, had spent two days scouting; he had seen a large buck and found a good place to set up a stand. During four days

Toby Bridges scouted this area and found sign indicating big bucks in the area. He stayed on his tree stand for several days without seeing a good-sized deer. Then, this giant whitetail crossed his path. Toby's scouting results gave him the confidence to stay on his stand in sub-zero weather.

of hunting in sub-zero weather, Toby did not see one shootable buck; however, he had confidence in the area he had scouted and refused to move. The next day he was rewarded with a giant 10-pointer. His scouting paid off in confidence and the confidence paid off in harvesting a big buck.

Various scouting techniques have worked for numerous hunters across the country. It is in every hunter's best interest to plan a strategy before the hunting season actually opens. Researching through personal contacts and reading materials, learning the terrain by planning a fly-over and examining topo maps and locating sign, such as shed antlers, are some important ingredients to a successful hunt.

About The Authors

Chuck Adams is an accomplished bowhunter with 45 official Pope and Young Club record-book animals. Chuck was the first bowhunter to harvest all 27 recognized North American big-game animals—a feat called the Super Slam.

His credits also include the four-species Grand Slam on wild sheep and a world-record Sitka black-tailed deer, as well as a world-record Coues' deer. He is the only bowhunter in history to bag three Grand Slams on deer.

At age 16, Chuck arrowed a forked horn Columbia black-tailed deer in northern California. That early success, combined with sound instruction from his father, began Chuck's lifelong love affair with bowhunting. Chuck is a full-time writer with more than 3,000 magazine articles published. He is the ''Bowhunting'' columnist for *North American Hunter*, and has written several books on bowhunting and archery. Chuck lives in Montana.

Tony Caligiuri is the Field Editor for *North American Hunter*. He is also the president of the Texas chapter of the International Black Powder Hunters Association. An Iowa native, Tony hunts all types of big game.

Tony has been an active freelance writer and photographer since his college journalism days. His work has appeared in more than 30 national and regional magazines. Tony is also the coauthor of the NAHC Hunter's Information Series book entitled *Modern Bird Hunting*.

Tony has harvested several record-book animals, including a desert bighorn sheep that won the prestigious Foundation for North American Wild Sheep's Gold Medal award and an SCI top-10 black bear that was a North American major award-winner.

An active member of the Outdoor Writers Association of America, Tony was featured in a 3M Sportsman Library video production on hunting Texas white-tailed deer. Tony lives in Texas and has hunted from the Arctic Circle to the interior of Mexico and in more than 20 states.

Ron Doss, a freelance writer and photojournalist, is a native of the Mississippi Delta, which is described by William Faulkner as "starting in the lobby of the Peabody Hotel in Memphis and ending on Catfish Row in Vicksburg, Mississippi." Ron learned to read when he was three years old, and the public library eventually became his afternoon babysitter.

His love for writing festered during a 25-year business and financial administration career. Then, he met Bern Keating, who has been described as "the greatest living writer of non-fiction." Bern helped Ron polish his writing skills and begin a new career.

Ron has written over 100 articles for many national and regional publications. He is the outdoor columnist for the *Northeast Mississippi Daily Journal*. A member of the Southeastern Outdoor Press Association, Ron received its prestigious "Excellence in Craft" award in 1991.

Ron lives in Tupelo, Mississippi, with his wife, Diane, and son, Kirby.

Bill Hanus built an advertising business in Chicago. He worked mostly for the publishing industry, handling several big names. Guns were not a part of his professional life at this point, but he was still a bird-shooter.

Bill eventually moved his family and business to Sante Fe, New Mexico; however, after 10 years of bi-weekly trips to Chicago, he withdrew from the industry altogether.

He then started a newsletter dealing with SKB shotguns. It eventually evolved into a trading post for guns—new and used. This prompted his interest and research into developing the best possible bird gun. The SKB went out of business, leaving a niche open for the kind of gun Bill liked and a newsletter without a purpose. Bill Hanus asked himself this question: If you could dream up the ideal gun for your kind of hunting and put it together using concepts from any era and design preferences from any country, what would it look like? The Bill Hanus Birdgun was the result.

Kevin Howard grew up on a farm in northeast Missouri. Over the last 20 years, he has seen a dramatic increase in deer numbers and hunting opportunities in his home state.

Kevin began outdoor writing in 1982 and started his own outdoor paper in St. Louis in 1983. He works for the Farrell Group, a public relations agency specializing in the outdoors market. His clients include Winchester Ammunition and Tasco Scopes.

Each year, he successfully hunts deer in several states, including Missouri, Illinois and Georgia. He also spends several days a year observing and scouting deer on his family farm.

Kevin is active with several conservation organizations at both the local and national level. He has been an active leader in educating the public about good habitat and game management.

Kevin and his wife, Elaine, live on a family farm north of St. Louis with their children, Erin and Andrew.

Mark LaBarbera is an award-winning writer, photographer, book author, magazine editor, publisher and all-around sportsman. His outdoor pursuits include adventures in Africa, South America, Central America, Canada and the United States. He hunts with both gun and bow.

Mark graduated from the University of Wisconsin and became a newspaper reporter. Within a short amount of time, he became an associate editor for a national bowhunting magazine. He later advanced to Editor and now Publisher of *North American Hunter*.

The combination of his journalism skills and love for the outdoors has helped Mark become a leader in promoting the pro-hunting message. Mark is an officer and director of the Outdoor Writers Association of America and belongs to or serves on boards of various hunting and outdoor-related organizations, as well as several other professional organizations.

Bill Miller's earliest hunting recollection is being licked to submission at a tender age by a litter of his dad's springer-spaniel puppies. Since then, he has followed those dogs over hill and dale chasing all kinds of upland birds and waterfowl. Bill has hunted in states across the Midwest, West and South for big game and birds. He has also hunted in Canada and Mexico.

Bill is a graduate of the University of Wisconsin-Eau Claire with a degree in journalism and an emphasis in environmental communication. During his studies, Bill hosted, produced, wrote, filmed and edited the "Chippewa Valley Outdoors" television series. Bill is Editor of *North American Hunter*; he has also authored chapters for the Hunter's Information Series books *Modern Bird Hunting* and *Successful Hunting Strategies*.

Bill is an active member of the Outdoor Writers Association of America and the Association of Great Lakes Outdoor Writers.

Hal Swiggett has been writing for over 45 years with more than 3,000 articles published in various firearms journals. From his San Antonio office, he edits several firearms publications and writes many magazine columns, including a handgun column for *North American Hunter*. Hal also wrote two chapters for the Hunter's Information Series book *Successful Hunting Strategies*.

Hal was named "Outstanding American Handgunner" in 1982, which inducted him into the American Handgunner Hall of Fame in the National Firearms Museum in Washington, D.C. In 1990, he was named Anschutz/Precision Sales Gun Writer of the Year. In 1991, he was inducted into the Handgun Hunter's Hall of Fame in Mt. Clemens, Michigan, and he received the first Lifetime Cicero award from the National Association of Federally Licensed Firearms Dealers, as well as the St. Gabriel Possenti Medal. Hal was chairman of the Outstanding American Handgunner Awards Foundation and now serves as its president. He also serves on the board of directors for the National Firearms Museum.

Larry Weishuhn is one of the country's most respected professional wildlife biologists and outdoor writers. As a biologist, he has established quality deer management programs on well over 10 million acres throughout North America.

Larry has been responsible for the production of numerous award-winning outdoor videos and appears occasionally on outdoor television shows, such as "North American Outdoors." A prolific writer, his work appears in various outdoor publications, including *North American Hunter* where he serves on the Shooting Advisory Council. He has authored two books, *Pear Flat Philosophies* and *Mostly Deer Hunting*, and contributed chapters to numerous others.

Larry has hunted deer from just below Canada's tundra to Mexico's arid brushlands. Because of his extensive work and hunting of white-tailed deer, he has been referred to in numerous publications as "Mr. Whitetail."

Duane Wiltse has been guiding and outfitting professionally since 1974. His three Wyoming wilderness camps control nearly 200 square miles of prime Rocky Mountain bighorn sheep, trophy bull elk and massive mule deer habitat. One camp, Camp Monaco, is a national historical site; it was established in the late 1800s by none other than Buffalo Bill Cody himself.

In Montana, Colorado and New Mexico, Duane has broadened his knowledge and expertise with summer pack trips, corporate retreats, wildlife consulting and ranch management. He says these projects are challenging and rewarding, but nothing compares to outfitting clients for big game in Wyoming's high wild grizzly country. Icy horse trails, ornery pack mules and camp-raiding grizzlies provide Duane with material for his adventure stories, four of which are in the NAHC book *Guides' Tales of Adventure*.

A Life Member of NAHC, Duane has donated hunts for membership drives and is an NAHC Approved outfitter and guide.

John Woods is director of the North American Hunting Club's Shooting Advisory Council. This council is set up to answer all firearms questions from NAHC Members. John thoroughly understands firearms and hunting firsthand. His knowledge stems from over 30 years of personal hunting experience in North America and Canada. He owns an extensive firearms reference library and is a prolific reader on the subjects of firearms history, development and application —all for the sport of hunting.

John operated a gun business for years and became an official NRA firearms appraiser. He is also a certified hunter safety instructor. A freelance writer and columnist, John is an active member of the Outdoor Writers Association of America. He is a Life Member of North American Hunting Club, as well as several other outdoor and sports organizations. He earned a doctorate in industrial psychology and a master's degree in wildlife science from Missouri University. John lives in Mississippi.

Don Zutz is a former high school Latin and English teacher who left the classroom in 1970 for a full-time career in freelance writing. Besides a master's degree from the University of Wisconsin, Don has a lifetime of handloading and wingshooting experience with forays into big-game hunting and varminting. He answers questions regularly in *North American Hunter*'s "Shooting Q & A" column.

Don is the author of six books about handloading, shotguns and shotgunning. He also authored a cookbook, covering wild-game recipes.

As a competitive shotgunner, Don has won two state skeet championships and numerous other events, as well as the hunter event at the national sporting clays championship. His hunting travels have taken him from South America to Canada, from Chesapeake Bay to Idaho. He has also visited many sporting arms and ammunition plants. Don lives in Kohler, Wisconsin.

Index